MONTMARTRE

MONTMARTRE

Translated by Anne Carter

Philippe Jullian

PHAIDON OXFORD

Phaidon Press Limited, Littlegate House, St Ebbe's Street, Oxford

Published in the United States of America by E. P. Dutton & Co., Inc.

First published in 1977
© 1977 by Phaidon Press Limited
All rights reserved
ISBN 0 7148 1712 0
Library of Congress Catalog Card Number: 76-5353

Filmset and printed in Great Britain by
BAS Printers Limited, Wallop, Hampshire

CONTENTS

1
SHRINES

Concerning its etymology, historians disagree: to some, Montmartre is Mons Martis, the Mount of Mars, to others it is Mons Mercurii, the Mount of Mercury. There was probably a small Gallic shrine on the wooded hill, beside a spring – Montmartre still had three springs up until the beginning of the last century. And, as always, the Gallic divinity took on a Roman name and continued to attract a scattering of worshippers: the men who cultivated the vineyards on the south-facing slopes of the hill, the smallholders whose fields ran down to the River Seine. From the summit of Montmartre watchers saw the arrival of the Germanic hordes that crossed the ill-defended Rhine in A.D. 272 and swept across Gaul, burning and pillaging. After their passing, Lutetia (Paris), which had covered a large area of the left bank, shrank to the Île de la Cité and the stones of the broken monuments were used to build up its walls.

Some time after this disaster – the precise date is uncertain but there is no doubt that there was such a person – a man named Denys or Dionysius was sent to convert that part of Gaul to Christianity. With him came Rusticus, a priest, and a deacon, Eleutherius. Two streets in Montmartre are named after them. They were so well received by the local inhabitants that the authorities took fright and, backed by the decrees of the Emperor Diocletian, arrested them. Here legend takes over from history. They were taken to Montmartre and ordered to sacrifice before the altar of Mars (or Mercury). The missionaries' refusal resulted in their execution, hence the third derivation, Mons Martyrum, or Martyrs' Mount. Decapitation put an end to Denys's sufferings, whereupon he picked up his head and carried it down to the plain, to a point some two or three miles north of his place of execution, thereafter known as Saint-Denis, where he was buried. This type of miracle, known as cephalophoria, is a great hagiographic rarity. The legend was exploited several hundred years later by the monks of Saint-Denis, who tended the tomb erected to the martyr by the last Merovingians. The church was rebuilt magnificently by the first Capetian kings, who were also buried there. Meanwhile, every seven years until the Revolution, the monks of Saint-Denis climbed Montmartre in solemn procession, bearing relics, to the place where their patron saint had been beheaded, thus acknowledging the spiritual pre-eminence of the hill known as the Butte. One year they did try to get out of the duty, on the excuse that it was raining, but the abbess, a La Rochefoucauld, said up they must go, they would have seven years to get dry.

St Denis had become so much a part of French mythology that in 1875, when the government of the Third Republic decided to adorn the walls of the Panthéon with pictures recalling the nation's legendary origins, it asked Bonnat to paint St Denis picking up his head. It is one of the best examples of French official art. Puvis de Chavannes, too, painted the story of St Genevieve, who must also have gone up to Montmartre to watch for the approach of the barbarian hordes.

The early Christians gathered the martyrs' remains into a cave on the side of the hill and developed the habit of burying their own dead alongside the holy bones,

Abbey of Montmartre in 1625. The church of Saint-Pierre is on the right turning the place into a miniature catacomb. Centuries passed and although the bulk of the worshippers departed to worship St Denis at a richer shrine, the passion of the people of Paris for their favourite saint gave rise to other pilgrimages. A chapel called the Martyrium was erected half-way up, on the site of the cave which may well have been one of the earliest gypsum mines. The various parishes of the capital would journey across country to it, each at a different time of year. That Montmartre was a place of especial veneration during the Dark Ages is clear from the fact that in 978 the Emperor Otto II, at war with King Lothair (a descendant of Charlemagne), celebrated his sweeping victories with a tremendous 'Halleluja' at the top of the hill which could be heard as far as Paris.

In 1133 Louis VI became the owner of the sacred mount. He built a parish church there and, at the instigation of his wife, Queen Adelaide, founded an abbey of nuns around the martyrs' chapel. The church, dedicated to St Peter, occupied the top of the hill: it was consecrated on 21 April 1147 by Pope Eugenius III and St Bernard, abbot of Clairvaux, which indicates the importance attached to the shrine. Saint-Pierre de Montmartre is therefore the oldest church in Paris. Notre-Dame was not begun until 1160. It is one of the earliest churches in which Gothic arches were used – the Gothic style is believed to have originated in the north of the Île de France, at Saint-Denis and Morienval. Saint-Pierre is a largish church, very much restored. Indeed, in 1850 it was in such a bad state that Merimée, who was inspector of historical monuments, recommended pulling it down. Somehow, it stood up for another thirty years, when it was thoroughly restored. With its plain seventeenth-century façade and modest tower, Saint-Pierre de Montmartre is the kind of monument that has more to offer the archaeologist than the casual visitor, impressed merely by its antiquity. Scholars are intrigued by the four black marble columns on either side of the organ. They are surmounted by later Gallo-Roman capitals and appear to serve a decorative purpose, even though they are in deep shadow. The boldest assert that they supported the ancient Temple of Mars (or Mercury), others that they adorned a Merovingian palace. Montmartre is mentioned frequently in the *chansons de geste*, but only in passing and as one shrine among many on the way to St James of Compostella, and then the reference is to the martyrs' chapel tended by the Benedictines, which was only opened at times of pilgrimage, and not to the parish church.

On 15 August 1534 a very great event took place in this little chapel, before the altar of the martyrs. A young Basque priest, a student at the Sorbonne, Ignatius de Loyola, collected several friends together there and swore a solemn oath to serve the Roman Catholic Church, to combat the spread of heresy and spread the true faith throughout the world by means of a semi-secret organization which was to be called the Society of Jesus. After making the vow, Ignatius and his companions, one of whom was the future St Francis Xavier, went to the fountain of St Denis on the north side of the hill where there was an inn for pilgrims. They spent the day drawing up the rules of the new society. Ignatius knew Montmartre well because he would go into retreat in the more or less abandoned quarries which had mined the hill since Roman times. They reminded him of the caves in the Thebaid where the first hermits had taken refuge. The Jesuits do not seem to have retained any particular feeling for Montmartre as the birthplace of their order, possibly because they have never been very popular in France. There is nothing to remind one of the splendours of the Gésù in Rome, the Gesuiti in Venice or the extravagant buildings of the Monastery of Loyola.

In the sixteenth century, the church of Saint-Pierre was first and foremost the church of a powerful abbey whose lands, enriched by a variety of gifts, stretched as far as Clichy in the west, southwards to the present Gare Saint-Lazare and eastwards to the Gare du Nord, in other words, over the whole northern suburbs of medieval Paris. The abbey buildings covered the whole of the top of the Butte. The Benedictine nuns were known as the 'Dames de Montmartre' and their convent existed for more than seven hundred years, that is, with various ups and downs, until the Revolution. The nuns acquired a collection of relics to attract pilgrims: the skulls of St Arnulf, Bishop of Metz, and of St Catherine of Sweden, a tooth belonging to St Armine, the daughter of St Dagobert II, King of Austrasia, a number of bones from the Eleven Thousand Virgins, a piece of St Joseph's cloak, and a great many more donated by pious visitors and kept in rich reliquaries.

The 'Ladies of Montmartre' frequently had a reputation for levity. Piety and gallantry went hand in hand on the sacred hill. Catherine of Clermont, sister of Diane de Poitiers, was their most outstanding abbess in the sixteenth century, and she re-established an order which was to be disrupted again twenty years later by the wars of religion. Soldiers hostile to the Protestant Henri IV quartered themselves in the abbey, and the resulting confusion may be imagined. After remarking that 'Paris was worth a mass', Henri IV prepared for his entry into the capital by lighting an immense bonfire in front of the church of Saint-Pierre where he had just heard a Te Deum. Soon afterwards he decided to reorganize the royal abbey of Montmartre and put Marie de Beauvilliers at its head. This remarkable woman won back the enthusiasm (and the donations) of the people of Paris by restoring the chapel of the martyrs, which had fallen into great disrepair. In 1611, during the course of this work, a cave was discovered, filled with bones which could only have been those of the martyred St Denys and his companions. A new chapel was erected and soon splendid buildings replaced the old monastery, with extensive gardens looking over Paris. Once a year the Chapter of Notre-Dame came in solemn procession to pray at the martyrs' chapel. It meant prosperity for the community and for the village clustered round its walls. Henri IV himself had a love nest, the Château Rouge, at the eastern end of the Butte, where the Boulevard Barbès is today.

Its proximity to the capital, fresh air and prioresses drawn from the noblest families attracted ladies of quality, both for short stays and to spend their old age in

Telegraph tower built on the church of Saint-Pierre, about 1850

good company. They were able to rent apartments, which increased the income of the nuns still more. Most notable of these ladies was a cousin of Louis XIV, the daughter of Gaston d'Orléans and separated from her husband Cosimo, Grand Duke of Tuscany. Her temperamental nature and her escapades provided Saint-Simon with many a salty episode in his memoirs. The first of Montmartre's shocking characters, she sought to ingratiate herself with the nuns by bringing with her a relic of no mean order: the complete and perfectly preserved corpse of a Blessed Florentine.

The streets of Montmartre and those leading up to it preserve the memory of the abbey in such names as the Place des Abbesses. The Boulevard Rochechouart and the Rue La Rochefoucauld recall the mother superiors who came from those families. The superior in 1792 was a Montmorency. An old woman, nearly blind, she saw her community broken up, its valuables seized and its furniture sold. Attempts to hide her were in vain and she was executed on the eve of Robespierre's fall. And so two severed heads, those of St Denis and of its last abbess, mark the beginning and the end of Montmartre's history as a religious site, a span of fourteen centuries.

2
WINDMILLS, CABARETS AND QUARRIES

The processions, pilgrimages and fairs which grew up around the shrine were not the only source of wealth for the inhabitants of the village that clustered round the walls of the Benedictine abbey. From early medieval times, windmills had multiplied on the summit of the Butte. The grain was brought up from the rich plains stretching to the north and the bakers came from Paris for the flour, whence there was a continual traffic with relays to enable the draught horses to reach the top of the hill. Windmills are already to be seen on Parisian miniatures of the fourteenth century: the oldest, called the Radet, later famous as the Moulin de la Galette, dates from 1292. (It was moved in 1923.) There are windmills to be seen on the skyline in old maps of the capital. As their numbers grew they became as inseparable as the martyrs from the minds of Parisians when they thought of Montmartre. The poet Regnard, in the reign of Louis XIII, sang of the hill:

> Where thirty windmills with their sails outspread
> Tell me each day what wind drives overhead.

Tasso, who came to Paris in Cardinal d'Este's train, remembered far from kindly those windmills 'that turn as fast as the Parisians' heads'. In short, they became so much the emblem of Montmartre that when Louis XVI's brother, the Comte de Provence, set up his porcelain factory on the side of the Butte, under the name of Clignancourt, he chose a windmill for its mark.

There were vines, too, belonging to the Benedictine ladies, but their wine was thin and kept badly and was drunk only in the *guinguettes*, those places of refreshment, music and dancing, which, in the eighteenth century and after, began to spring up along all the roads going up to the church of Saint-Pierre. Plenty more vineyards supplied these establishments, because, lying outside the walls of the capital, it was possible to drink wine there without paying tax. The octroi wall which had the name of the Fermiers Généraux only took in the foot of Montmartre: it ran along the boulevards of Clichy and Rochechouart without touching Montmartre itself and every drunkard in the capital could go and get drunk on the cheap outside the walls, on the pretence that they could sit out of doors and be out in the country, after all. As a result it was not long before a reputation for licence began to compete with the aura of sanctity.

Its reputation was so bad that very few aristocrats or financiers built '*petites maisons*' there to house their mistresses. Montmartre was the preserve of the commonalty, if not actually of the riff-raff. But some members of the lesser bourgeoisie, like the father of Louis XIV's court poet Boileau, had farms there where they spent the summer months. Another of these was the actor, Rose de Rosimont, who took over Molière's parts at his death. The porch and garden of his house are still there, at 12 Rue Cortot, and, as we shall see, many famous artists lived there. The cabarets, which often partook of the brothel, were hung with signs that spoke for themselves: they had names like La Fontaine d'Amour, Le Caprice des Dames, Le Berger Galant

The day after the storming of the Bastille, when the National Guard took cannons up to Montmartre to use them against the forces of law and order

– but the most notorious of them all was called Aux Armes de Madame l'Abbesse.

Towards the end of the eighteenth century, gardens in the same style as the famous Vauxhall Gardens in London, where there were cafés, theatres and dancing, sprang up all around the capital. There were several on the slopes of Montmartre. The oldest was at the top of the Rue Saint-Lazare: its founders were the famous firework manufacturers, the Ruggieri brothers, and fireworks were naturally the chief attraction, lighting up the sky over Paris on summer nights. Later on they installed the *montagnes russes*, which were the forerunners of the modern scenic railway. After the Egyptian campaign, during the Consulate, there was a Delta garden which must have borne a strong resemblance to a stage set for *The Magic Flute*, but its popularity

Barrière Blanche by Ledoux. Late eighteenth-century engraving

Barrière Blanche

(*right*) Corot: *Moulin de la Galette*, 1840. Geneva, Musée d'Art et d'Histoire

was short-lived. The tradition of these gardens carried on into the restoration of the monarchy with the Nouveau Tivoli, but only one example now remains in Europe, the Tivoli in Copenhagen. The Nouveau Tivoli was run by a Scotsman, the celebrated illusionist, Robertson. There were fountains, a hall of wonders, a pigeon shoot and, on occasion, a balloon ascension. Robertson's tomb in the cemetery of Père Lachaise has a bas-relief depicting phantasmagoric scenes. Long afterwards there was a Cabaret de L'Enfer in the Boulevard de Clichy in the same vein.

Revolution and Empire brought little interruption to the chief industry of the people of Montmartre, for the Parisians were still able to find cheaper wine there and to slake their thirst with it whenever patriotic fervour took them to the Butte. As on

Cabaret of Ramponeau, meeting-place for disreputable boys. Early eighteenth-century engraving

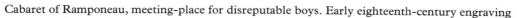

(*left*) Sisley: *Vue de Montmartre*, 1869. Musée de Grenoble

the occasion after the Fourteenth of July when the National Guard hauled cannon up to the top of Montmartre, with no very clear idea of whether they meant to use them to fire on the royalist troops, if Louis XVI should try to avenge the taking of the Bastille, or to disperse the twenty thousand or so unemployed, vagrants and cut-throats who had been herded together in workhouses to labour in the quarries, but who had turned out to be first and foremost a source of trouble. Lafayette went up to Montmartre twice in order to harangue these poor wretches and get them to disperse. The convent, as we have seen, was broken up and for some time afterwards Montmartre became known as Mont Marat. Those who purchased the property of the Ladies of Montmartre were for the most part building contractors who promptly set about quarrying the sacred hill.

There had always been quarries on Montmartre. As early as the sixteenth century there was a saying that there was more of Montmartre in Paris than Paris in Montmartre. The gypsum from Montmartre was so fine that it was used to make an imitation alabaster. Plaster of Paris is, in fact, plaster of Montmartre. But the quarriers were not entitled to undermine the monastery buildings or gardens, so new owners of the state property made haste to pull down the buildings, with the exception of the parish church, and put up lime kilns in the ruins. They dug quite

The gardens of the Château Rouge in 1854 surrounding the seventeenth-century building

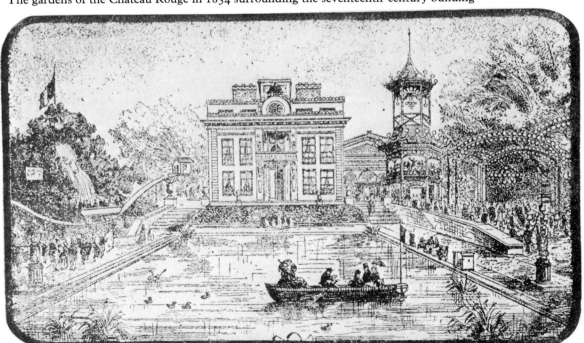

regardless; houses collapsed and one day an entire wedding party, dancing in the garden of a *guinguette*, vanished into a subterranean gallery. Three of the drinking fountains that were the charm of Montmartre were polluted. These deep mysterious quarries, their ramifications extending over several levels, became a refuge for cut-throats; under Louis XV magicians celebrated strange rites in them. Marat fled there from the king's police in 1789 and the bodies of the Swiss Guards, who were the last defenders of the monarchy, were thrown pell-mell into one of the quarries after the massacre of 10 August 1792. Until the middle of the nineteenth century the entrance was by way of three enormous blocked arches, where the steps leading up to the Sacré-Cœur are today. The effect of these labyrinths on the Romantics can be imagined. 'There was a quarry by the Château Rouge that looked like a druidical temple with its flat lintels supported on lofty pillars: the eye was drawn into depths where one trembled to see the formidable gods of our fathers,' wrote Gérard de Nerval. The numerous cabarets frequented by the quarrymen had a bad reputation.

The indiscriminate excavations which took place during the Empire gave science a new branch: palaeontology. Indeed, it was in one of these new quarries that they found the bones which enabled Cuvier to make his reconstructions of prehistoric animals. The first known dinosaurs and archaeopteryx came from Montmartre.

South-east view of the Butte. Lithograph of about 1820

Napoleon was alarmed at the state of Montmartre. A point of strategic importance both to check an enemy advancing from the north and to threaten Paris in the event of an insurrection could not be allowed to collapse. He had some idea of setting up a beacon in place of the semaphore tower, then, since he always had a flair for exploiting old beliefs, the emperor seriously considered the possibility of erecting a Temple of Peace on the martyrs' hill, a splendid monument to dominate his capital. In the end he decided to go to Montmartre himself, strode swiftly through the wretched streets leading to the quarries, decided that they must be closed and demanded a broad, paved road to run from the Barrière Blanche to the top of the Butte, to be called the Rue de l'Empereur. It became, more modestly, the Rue Lepic.

The defeats of 1814 brought all these fine plans to nothing. On March 30 four hundred volunteers hauled guns up to the top and dug themselves in there. At the Château Rouge, to the east, Napoleon's brother Joseph, the ex-king of Spain, tried to organize some sort of resistance against the Russian forces until he learnt of the abdication. On the other side, at the Barrière de Clichy, General Moncey was trying desperately to defend Paris. A monument, still standing, was erected during the Second Empire to commemorate this battle. The Russians attacked Montmartre, shot the miller, Debray, dismembered him and hung the pieces from the sails of his mill. But the pleasure gardens and the *guinguettes* were very soon open again to welcome the allied soldiers. The English bivouacked on the heights and the soldiers

Michel: *View of Montmartre.* Louvre, Cabinet des Dessins

got indigestion from eating unripe grapes – poor consolation for the owners who lost their crops. For more than fifty years after that there were no more guns on Montmartre, but the vines were to vanish very quickly thanks to the developers, and the windmills to become purely ornamental, just part of the pastoral setting which the romantics succeeded in preserving in Montmartre into the reign of Louis-Philippe.

This revolutionary and even then romantic Montmartre had its painter, the first real painter belonging to the Butte. He was, naturally, a bohemian. Georges Michel (1763–1843) was an ardent revolutionary and a great lover, which did not prevent him cherishing a platonic affection for Madame Vigée-Lebrun. He had no time for painters who must have Italy: Montmartre, with its quarries, windmills and sunken roads was quite enough for him. He was an admirer of Rembrandt and the Dutch painters. Some of his skies have the same beauty as Ruysdael's and his trees can be as romantic as Hobbema's ancient oaks. Georges Michel's purchasers were lovers of Dutch painting. For several years he kept a junk shop in the Rue de Cléry which served him as a studio. Then, on fine days, he would go up to the Butte, followed by his wife and a donkey loaded with his painting gear. Georges Michel was a forerunner of the masters of the Barbizon school, but he cannot be said to have influenced them because he was little known in his lifetime. The same posthumous fame was to be the lot of many of the painters who succeeded him on the Butte.

3
ROMANTIC STROLLS

In spite of the speculators and the encroaching quarries, Montmartre remained the closest village to Paris. One could walk up there in half an hour from the *grands boulevards*. Smart folk went in their carriages to Auteuil or Neuilly but the *petits bourgeois* preferred Montmartre and if they felt tired they could hire donkeys to carry them to the top from the Barrière de Clichy. The village kept the comic opera charm which its bailiff in the days of Louis XV had wanted for it. It could have been the setting for Rousseau's *Le Devin du Village*. Some of the drinking fountains had been polluted by the quarries but there were enough left to attract strollers and lovers, and they had been bowered in trees to draw the Parisians. By 1830 the trees had grown very tall but the fountains were decaying. Nerval sought there recollections of his childhood impressions in the Valois:

I dwelt for a long time in Montmartre, where one enjoys very pure air, varied prospects and can behold magnificent views, whether 'having been virtuous, one likes to see the sunrise', which is very beautiful over Paris, or, having less simple tastes, prefers the empurpled colours of sunset, where the drifting fragments of cloud paint scenes of battle and transfigurations above the great cemetery, in between the Arc de l'Etoile and the blue-tinted hills that go from Argenteuil to Pontoise. The new houses are advancing all the time, like the diluvian sea that washed the sides of the ancient mountain, gaining little by little on the lairs that were the refuge of the formless monsters since reconstructed by Cuvier. Assailed on one side by the Rue de l'Empereur and on the other by the *quartier de la mairie*, which is undermining the steep slopes and shaving off the heights on the Paris side, the old mount of Mars will soon share the fate of the Butte des Moulins, which, in the last century, showed scarcely less proud a face. Nevertheless, we still have left some hillsides bounded by thick green hedges which the barberry decks by turns with its purple flowers and its dark red berries.

There are windmills, cabarets and arbours, rustic paradises and quiet lanes, bordered with cottages, barns and bushy gardens, green fields ending in cliffs where springs filter through the clay, gradually cutting off certain small islands of green where goats frisk and browse on the thistles that grow out of the rocks; proud, surefooted little girls watch over them, playing amongst themselves. You may even find a vine, last of the famous Montmartre vintage which from Roman times vied with Argenteuil and Suresnes. Year by year, this humble hillside loses another row of its stunted rootstocks as they topple into a quarry. Ten years ago, I could have bought it for three thousand francs – today they are asking thirty thousand. It is the finest view to be had anywhere near Paris.

What attracted me in this small space sheltered by the great trees of the Château des Brouillards, was first of all this remnant of a vineyard, bound up with the memory of St Denis, who, from a philosopher's point of view, was

Mimi Pinson's house

Tomb of Berlioz. Berlioz spent his early married years in Montmartre

possibly a second Bacchus, and who had three bodies, one of which was buried in Montmartre, the second at Ratisbon and the third in Corinth. Next to that, it was the presence of the drinking trough which is enlivened every evening with the sight of horses and dogs being watered, and of a fountain built in the antique style where the washerwomen gossip and sing as they do in the opening chapters of *Werther*. Given a bas-relief of Diana and perhaps a pair of naiad faces carved in half-relief, with the shade of the old lime trees that overhang the monument, one would have an admirable and for much of the time an undisturbed retreat, reminiscent in some ways of the Roman Campagna. (*Promenades et Souvenirs*)

Gérard de Nerval stayed several times in Montmartre, with Théophile Gautier in the Rue de Navarin in 1840, and later on we find him stopping briefly in the Rue Pigalle and the Rue des Martyrs. In 1841, when he felt his madness coming on, he went for eight months to Dr Esprit Blanche for treatment. Not a very strict cure: the poet was able to spend whole nights rambling about the Butte. He found the workers from the quarries and other prowlers gathered round huge fires:

There are only two habitable quarries left today, near Clignancourt. But they are filled with workers, half of them asleep, ready to relieve the others later on. And so the colour is lost!

A thief can always find a bed: those picked up in the quarries were generally only honest vagrants who dared not seek shelter at the station or drunkards coming down the hill, unable to drag themselves any further.

Round about Clichy there are sometimes enormous gas pipes, left lying outside ready for later use because they are impossible to carry away. These were the vagabonds' last refuge after the closing of the great quarries. Five or six of them would emerge from the pipes, one after another. You had only to bang one end with a rifle butt.   (*Les Nuits d'Octobre*)

Then came a character who inspired a century of poets, novelists and composers of operettas, the working-class Parisienne and friend of artists, Mimi Pinson. Alfred de Musset gave her her name and declared her a republican at heart. She lives in an attic but her window is filled with flowers. Mimi Pinson is a milliner or a seamstress, singing in the wilderness the songs of Béranger or Nadaud; she plays, in short, in the facile poetry of the romantics, the part of the shepherdess in eighteenth-century songs. After the Revolution, it was no longer the countryside but the world of the working class on which sensitive spirits would dwell tenderly. Victor Hugo's *Les Misérables* is the best example of this interest, although the *Mystères de Paris* by Eugène Sue are much more exciting. Mimi Pinson is a sister of Murger's Mimi. *La Vie de Bohème* belongs essentially to the left bank. Thirty or forty years later, the artists and the girls of Montmartre re-enacted the touching incidents of the *Vie de Bohème* over and over again. Mimi Pinson had had lovers, but all for love. Her sister,

(*above*) Moulin de la Galette. Lithograph, about 1820

(*below*) View of Paris from Montmartre. The engraving was made for the English tourists who came to Paris under the Consulate

(*above right*) The Moulin de la Galette in about 1840

(*below right*) The Moulin de la Galette in about 1860. Watercolour by le Fèvre in the Musée du Vieux Montmartre

the *grisette*, had lovers too, but most of them paid. She usually lived at the foot of Montmartre, in the district of Notre-Dame de Lorette, whence the other nickname the *Lorettes*, and she would go up to Montmartre to meet her real friends. The romantic *guinguettes* were to be exploited fifty years later. Every tiny cabaret garden did its best to reproduce the operatic setting with trellises and swings. Willette, a facile artist but not without a certain verve, drew scenes of Mimi Pinson dancing with pierrots among the windmills. The burgeoning of the pseudo-rustic had begun.

Lorettes and *grisettes* have been depicted a hundred times over by Gavarni, a remarkably clever, commonplace artist considered by the Goncourts to be the Watteau of the nineteenth century. That is an exaggeration. But there is a dark side to Gavarni's lithographs which is interesting: men prowling, club in hand, in a sunken road; drunkards slumped against a wall; two ruffians muttering together under a dead tree ... the heroes of the *Mystères de Paris*. The background, sketchily indicated, belongs to a disturbing Montmartre of half-built houses, cabarets of varying degrees of rusticity and dead-end streets of a more or less murderous appearance.

The Goncourts have said a good deal about the area which young Gavarni was sketching in 1830 or thereabouts. 'Picturesque sketches of the half-wild Montmartre of that time, its mine buildings, crumbling cottages, sinister quarry entries and the beauties of the fences round the waste ground that were to become the background of his later lithographs; the abandoned corners, filled with brambles, rubble and nettles, that would be trodden by the barefoot bohemians of the suburbs in his later works.' During the reign of Louis-Philippe, Gavarni had a studio in the Rue Blanche where he entertained on the nights of the Opéra balls. Everyone dressed at his house, he had a whole stock of fancy dresses, and then piled into carriages to go down to Paris, shouting and blowing horns. Yet there is a slightly sleazy side to the gaiety in Gavarni's lithographed scenes, reminding us of the two prisons waiting hard by for the unwary of Montmartre: the debtors' prison at Clichy and the gloomy Saint-Lazare, the women's prison, at the bottom of the Butte.

By 1840 Montmartre was decidedly more suburban than rural, in spite of its windmills and its tree-shaded streets. The church of Saint-Pierre was decaying slowly in its little graveyard where that curious character, Madame Swetchine, a sort of worldly mystic who at one time acquired a great influence over Tsar Alexander I, was buried.

Even so, the abbey ruins, the quarries and the abandoned fountains enabled artists who lacked the means to visit Rome to imagine themselves on the Palatine, and on fine days there was a deal of sketching on the Butte. In 1820 Géricault came to live in the Chaussée des Martyrs, next door to the painter Carle Vernet, who portrayed, in a long-celebrated canvas, the resistance at the Porte de Clichy. Géricault had a fall from his horse at the Barrière des Martyrs (the present Place Pigalle) and died of it on 21 January 1824. He would often go to draw the big horses pulling the carts filled

Troyon: *The descent from Montmartre*. The north side about 1835

with gypsum and his picture, the *Four à Plâtre*, was painted from these sketches. The sombre, sulphurous canvas shows us a sinister side of the Butte. The landscape painters, however, preferred the forest of Fontainebleau and the real village of Barbizon to the village of Montmartre. Millet, in 1845, had a wretched studio in the Rue Rochechouart: his first commission was to paint a shop sign for a draper's in the Rue Saint-Lazare. Troyon lived near the abattoirs whose place has been taken by the Collège Rollin: there he acquired a taste for drawing animals. Diaz de la Peña and the elegant Alfred de Dreux shared a studio in Montmartre for a time. A friend of Victor Hugo's, Auguste de Chatillon, a bad painter and a worse poet, lived for a long

Géricault: *Le Four à plâtre*, 1821–2. Paris, Louvre

time in the Rue des Tilleuls. Corot never lived in Montmartre, but he took his easel there more than once, along with the large blue umbrella that shielded him from the sun, when he could not get out into the real country. He painted the Moulin de la Galette and the narrow Rue Saint-Vincent, almost a village street, which has not changed so very much since 1850 when the picture was painted. Both were subjects repeated tirelessly by generations of painters.

The first major artist to live in Montmartre was Hector Berlioz, in 1833, not long after his marriage to the English actress Harriet Smithson. The house, 4 Rue du Mont-Cenis, was charming: two-storeyed, with green shutters and a patch of garden with one large tree, just the thing to make anyone happy who did not happen to have Berlioz's melancholic temperament, was not harassed by creditors and had not realized too late that his beloved was frigid. In spite of these drawbacks, the young couple appeared happy enough for several months. In their garden in the spring they entertained Liszt, Chopin, Alfred de Vigny, Alexandre Dumas, Eugène Sue and

Corot: *Rue Saint-Vincent*. Lyon, Musée des Beaux-Arts

Rue Saint-Vincent in about 1900

Théophile Gautier, six of whose poems, published under the title *Nuits d'Eté*, the composer wonderfully set to music. There, too, Berlioz wrote *Harold in Italy* and then the opera *Benvenuto Cellini*. After a few years, Berlioz went back to live in the *grands boulevards* that were the centre of life in Paris. Montmartre was all very well for lovers, but he was no longer one of them.

In 1840 Louis-Philippe's prime minister, Thiers, decided to incorporate all the communes lying immediately outside the defences constructed under Louis XVI into one huge system of fortifications. And so, although it did not become the eighteenth *arrondissement* until 1860, Montmartre at that time became to all intents a part of Paris. These fortifications were extremely costly, put a great deal into the minister's pockets and made it possible for Paris to sustain the frightful siege of the winter of 1870–1 and for the Commune to ferment in isolation.

But if, with the exception of Berlioz, the great romantics visited Montmartre only spasmodically, many of the most famous of them lie in the cemetery that was opened

(*right*) Van Gogh: *Le Moulin de la Galette*, 1886. Glasgow Art Gallery

in 1804 on the site of some old quarries and subsequently enlarged several times. Thus, in 1869, Berlioz found his way back to Montmartre for good. Alfred de Vigny had preceded him and Théophile Gautier was buried there in 1872. So were two elegant women who probably never ventured into Montmartre in their lives, Madame Récamier, the friend of Madame de Staël and inspiration of Chateaubriand, and Madame de Girardin, who had a brilliant *salon* in the time of Louis-Philippe. The most exquisitely unhappy of romantic poetesses, Marceline Desbordes-Valmore rests there, along with the most admirable classic tragedienne of the high romantic era, Rachel. Their graves are seldom visited. Stendhal, on the other hand, has a number of visitors, but the most flowers are always left on the grave of a little-known *demi-mondaine* called Alphonsine Plessis. For she was the model on whom Alexandre Dumas fils based *La Dame aux Camélias*. Later on, Offenbach, Meilhac, who wrote the librettos for his operettas, Renan and the Goncourt brothers were all buried in the cemetery of Montmartre. The weirdest tomb is that erected in 1890 by a M. Pigeon, the inventor of a kind of paraffin lamp. It shows the inventor's family, cast in bronze, illuminated by a lamp which for many years was piously kept alight by the custodians. The cemetery of Montmartre lacks the romantic charm of Père Lachaise. The rest of those who lie there must be somewhat disturbed by the traffic of the Rue Caulaincourt, which straddles the cemetery by means of a hideous iron bridge.

Renoir: *Moulin de la Galette*, 1876. Paris, Louvre

4
THE STUDIOS

In 1860, the commune of Montmartre became a district of Paris, the eighteenth *arrondissement*, extending considerably beyond the confines of the old Montmartre, since it took in the districts of Clignancourt and La Chapelle as far as the dismal outer boulevards along the fortifications. Montmartre remembered that tradition as well as geographical location made it a privileged place. The population had increased rapidly, from 2,000 round about 1800 to 30,000 in 1860, and the newcomers promptly adopted the spirit of Montmartre and displayed a degree of independence towards the habits and opinions of the capital. Who were these newcomers? People of modest means who felt that there was still something countrified in the old village streets, working people, because lodgings were cheap, and a good many prostitutes, for the Boulevard Rochechouart, named after an abbess from the celebrated family of the dukes of Mortemart, with its double row of trees planted on the site of the old walls, had quickly become a favourite haunt of theirs. Nowadays the Métro station Barbès-Rochechouart provides an incongruous connection with the revolutionary, Barbès, who has given his name to one of the perpendicular boulevards.

More and more artists set up their studios there, where the light was better than in the narrow streets of the left bank and rents cheaper than in the smart blocks on the Chaussée d'Antin where the fashionable painters lived. This district, known as the Nouvelle Athènes, had been built around 1830 on land which had once belonged to the abbey. Delacroix lived there for a long time, George Sand had a studio there, Degas and Gustave Moreau lived nearly all their lives in these straight streets, which were very far from picturesque but light and well built. Five minutes could take one down to the *grands boulevards* and the Opéra, but in five minutes, too, one could be across the octroi barrier and in a village: Montmartre.

Because of its altitude, Montmartre was still somewhat cut off. Grass grew between the paving stones, no omnibuses went up there and cabs would only venture upon promise of a large tip. The northern end of the Butte was still very poor and covered with waste ground given over to rag-and-bone men and to workers' dwellings as far as the gates of Clignancourt and La Chapelle. The uphill advance of the new buildings was quite slow and except for the streets built during the Restoration Montmartre in the Second Empire retained its rural aspect. There was still one country house, set in a large garden, with the romantic name of the Château des Brouillards, part of which was turned into a dance hall, and half a score of windmills. Some residences, more countrified than urban, held out for a long time against the developers. One such was the Louis XVI pavilion called the Boule d'Or on account of the metal ball on top. It belonged to a Baron Michel, who was mayor of Montmartre during a large part of the Second Empire. He was an art collector, the Barbizon school was well represented in his gallery, and there were also some Delacroixs. Baron Michel liked to entertain young artists and may have encouraged them to settle in his commune. Sisley, in 1869, gave the truest picture of this Montmartre, with the buildings climbing up to assail the greenery (*see opposite p. 15*).

Rue des Saules. A favourite subject for painters

Cheapness and fresh air were not the only reasons why young artists settled on this side of the walls: they were getting as far away as possible from the vicinity of the Institut and the Ecole des Beaux-Arts. Theoretically, Montmartre became something halfway between Paris and Barbizon. Courbet's friend, the critic Champfleury, wrote in 1860: 'Montmartre is a small provincial town at the gates of Paris, not unlike Pontoise: no traffic, no police, no people in the quiet streets, small houses set in gardens, little shops that smell of the country.' Guillaumin has left some charming canvases of it all.

The Romantic painters had loved the old houses and picturesque *quartiers*; their studios were like antique shops or the property rooms of the Opéra. Later on, the keynote of the studios that grew up on the hill, in gardens, stables and barns, was simplicity. The walls were hung with floral chintzes, a big divan bed covered in cushions, a few screens, and that was all. Friends, on the other hand, were a necessity, huge numbers of friends. Perhaps Courbet's vast picture of his studio, with Baudelaire, several hunters, women of all sorts and even a Persian, provided the model for this kind of artists' life. Montmartre was, above all else, a society of friends; everyone was in and out of each other's houses all the time and the girls went from one studio to another.

Montmartre had little in common with the Chelsea of the Pre-Raphaelites which was developing at much the same time. The Symbolists, thirty years later, with their intellectual intensity, their fatal muses and their drugs, provided a fair imitation of them. Montmartre in 1860 was nonconformist, but gay. Nonconformist it remained, even slavishly so, but by 1900 it was also somewhat sinister. It was in Montmartre that the cult of the artist, the artistic manner evolved from the writings of Baudelaire, developed. The artist had none of the preciosity of the Anglo-Saxon aesthete; he had a taste for Beauty, certainly, but he was free to find that beauty in scenes of misery and among the dregs of humanity. Incidentally, there was another reason why Montmartre became something of an asylum during the Second Empire. Paris, turned upside down by the works of Baron Haussmann, had lost much of its charm: from now on it became the financial capital which Zola depicted, and the artists took flight.

Baron Haussmann's works spared the sacred hill. There was indeed some talk, in 1857, of levelling it in order that building construction might not be impeded by the inequalities of the terrain, but happily the project came to nothing and sensibly the quarries were filled in with all the rubble from the demolition being carried out in the capital. And so the plaster of Paris which had played so great a part in its building returned at last to its quarries.

Who were the artists who settled in Montmartre during the Second Empire? An official painter like Thomas Couture had his studio there, but so did the landscape painter Jongkind. For half a century Ziem painted his sunsets over Venice in a curious building of vaguely Moorish design, and Puvis de Chavannes lived there, in

Manet: *Au café*, 1878. Winterthur, Oskar Reinhart Collection

(*overleaf*) Courbet: *The artist's studio*, 1855. Paris, Louvre

the Place Pigalle, from 1855 until his death in 1898, although his huge studio was at Neuilly and he was to be seen every morning, a most respectable gentleman, going down the Boulevard de Clichy on his way to paint his muses in classical settings. If he happened to meet Degas, the two would acknowledge one another coldly. Degas, who made no secret of the fact that he found Puvis's work insufferably tedious, lived on the other side of the Boulevard Rochechouart, in the Rue Victor Massé, and died in the Boulevard de Clichy. Puvis and Degas more than once used the same model, for instance the little Dobigny, who was the Hope in Puvis's most famous picture of that title, exhibited in the Salon of 1872. We find none of the same innocence when she poses for Degas.

A close friend of Degas's, Alfred Stevens, had several studios in Montmartre, in the Rue de Laval and later in the Rue Victor Massé and the Rue des Martyrs. The fair, handsome Belgian was worshipped by women and painted the elegant Parisiennes of 1860 to 1880 better than anyone. Stevens's smallest pictures sold for very high prices. He had a remarkable technique, very similar in the treatment of fabrics to that of Degas: later on he came under the influence of Manet and this was less successful. In his sumptuously furnished studio, Japanese art made its appearance, all mixed up with Louis XVI furniture and Flemish tapestries. He was fond of entertaining and Baudelaire could have been heard there, reading his translation of a story by Poe, while Alexandre Dumas fils observed the *demi-mondaines* posing for their portraits. Sarah Bernhardt, another of his models, borrowed ideas for the arrangement of her own studio in the *quartier* Monceau. Manet was a frequent visitor and painted more than one watercolour in the garden of the Rue des Martyrs. Stevens had opened a studio in the Boulevard Rochechouart which was frequented by society women, highly excited at the thought of going up to Montmartre. Then the fashion passed. Stevens, accustomed to living extravagantly, got into debt and by 1892, when he was an old man, he was obliged to make do with the meagre fare of the Rat Mort in the Place Pigalle, a haunt of young English painters.

> A magnificent old ruin, broad-shouldered, white-haired, with a fine head and a powerful frame, still erect in spite of his years. . . . A great lover of women, he had lived splendidly, he had been wildly extravagant and although he had once owned a whole street, he was now reduced to living in a modest atelier and a couple of rooms. . . . Still, everyone treated *le père Stevens* with great respect, for not only had he been a great figure, but he had been a great painter as well.
>   (William Rothenstein: *Men and Memories*)

Henner was another of the painters who settled in Montmartre. He painted red-haired Magdalens in landscapes overrun with pitch. For some time he had a studio in Montmartre, but when fame came to him he moved away and settled in the wealthy Plaine Monceau where one may still visit his museum. Many other painters went the same way after a success at the Salon, for it was important not to upset bourgeois clients by making them come to Montmartre, and so they would move into the smart districts or round about the Place Clichy, on the edge of Montmartre. Those who stayed in Montmartre felt that they were the purists, making fewer concessions to the world. Already there were not a few failures willing to make their purity an excuse for their lack of success.

Many young painters at that time were drawn by the presence of their seniors, but also by the literary reputation which naturalism was beginning to confer on Montmartre. *Germinie Lacerteux* by the Goncourt brothers, which came out in 1864, is the story of a fallen maidservant who roams Montmartre, haunting the dance halls (for the first time the outskirts of the city become the background for a work of literature), and is finally buried in the cemetery of Montmartre. Out of the landscape glimpsed over the cemetery wall, the brothers create the first Impressionist picture:

A few white rooftops stood out here and there, then the bulk of the Butte of Montmartre rose up, its shroud of snow rent by streaks of bare earth and patches of sand. Low grey walls followed the line of the hill, overtopped by scrawny trees, their branches looming purplish in the mist to where two black windmills stood. For light, there was a yellow brightness over Montmartre. Across this wintry gleam there passed again and again the sails of an invisible windmill, sails whose slow, regular circling was like the movement of eternity.

5
THE ELYSÉE~MONTMARTRE

The evolution of the *guinguettes* into the public dance halls which became so famous during the Second Empire had begun in the previous reign. The most celebrated of those in Montmartre was called the Elysée-Montmartre. The further away from the wealthy *quartiers*, the more extravagant and at the same time the more sordid these establishments became, with exotic palaces and gardens painted in *trompe-l'oeil* like booths at a fair. Yet this handbill of 1865 shows a distinct striving after splendour:

> A huge salon has been constructed in the garden, it has risen as if by magic and is quite unrivalled. It extends over an area of one thousand metres without a single supporting pillar, aerial galleries run round the walls, ending at an immense rock which is to form a platform for the orchestra; cascades and plantations of every kind add still more to the fairylike beauty of the edifice. A vast chalet with gaming rooms, a restaurant built with the most refined comfort, such are the innovations introduced by the proprietor, Mme Veuve Serre.

Entry was one franc on Sundays and seventy-five centimes on Mondays, Thursdays and Saturdays.

The Elysée-Montmartre, like the Boule Noire, was in the Boulevard Rochechouart, the Reine Blanche in the Boulevard de Clichy. Montmartre became the third pleasure centre of Paris, and the cheapest. The establishments in the Champs-Elysées, the Alcazar d'Eté or the Jardin de Paris, might be frequented by rich foreigners and dissipated aristocrats, the dance halls of the left bank, Mabille or the Closerie des Lilas, might be the haunts of students, but in Montmartre there lurked a more dangerous game, layabouts from Clichy or Belleville, workers from the slaughterhouses of La Vilette with a sprinkling of *petits bourgeois* in search of inexpensive enjoyment, errant Mimi Pinsons, young working girls or domestic servants looking for a change, and, hanging round them, a few pimps and madams out to enlarge their flocks. All these revolved under the rows of gas lamps against Moorish or rustic backgrounds, in the open air in summer but at other times in dance halls which, for all their lustre, had a somewhat barn-like air. The dances were polkas and waltzes. It was at the Boule Noire that the Lancers' quadrille, with figures daring enough to shock a Victorian ballroom, was danced for the first time. Next, they took up the quadrilles of Offenbach and it was to the music of *Orpheus in the Underworld* that the wild French cancan was born. It was originally called the chahut, as it was at the *bal de l'Opéra*, and it became the chief attraction of Montmartre in the nineties.

The stars of the Elysée-Montmartre at that period achieved European fame. There was Celeste Mogador, who imported the polka in 1848, and had a fine career in the *demi-monde* before becoming the Marquise de Chabrillan. Alongside this star, people were applauding the antics of other girls known simply by nicknames: Pomonne, Carabine, Rigolboche, Sabretache and Rose Pompon. These ladies were not strictly a *corps de ballet*; they would accept invitations from customers and leave

The quadrille at the Elysée-Montmartre. Drawing by Lunel in the *Courrier Français* in 1889

Garden of the Château Rouge. Lithograph of about 1850

them when their regulars required their attention, and, all together, they performed the famous chahut. In 1865, the proprietor of the Elysée-Montmartre engaged the celebrated conductor, Olivier Metra, one of whose waltzes, *La Vague*, is still remembered. He attracted a smarter type of customer to the place and the Elysée-Montmartre was still quite stylish by about 1875 when a young Englishman, George Moore, took there a girl friend, who was, rather reluctantly, about to follow a rich lover to Russia.

'The trees are beautiful,' she said, 'they are like a fairy tale;' and that is exactly what they were like, rising into the summer darkness, unnaturally green above the electric lights. In the middle of a circle of white globes the orchestra played upon an estrade, and every one whirled his partner as if she were a top. . . . The people rushed to see a quadrille; and while watching them I heard that a display of fire works was being arranged by special request. The news having got about that it was Marie's last night.

The Boule Noire, on the other hand, was going down. It had been opened during the Restoration by a one-time beauty nicknamed Belle Cuisse and retained a vaguely Pompeian décor, which Edmond de Goncourt copied for the production of the play based on his novel, *Germinie Lacerteux*:

> A corner of the ballroom of the Boule Noire with white walls, crude copies of Prudhon's *Saisons*, lit by triple gas jets reflected in mirrors and, at the doors and windows, drapes of crimson velvet trimmed with gold braid. The scene is set off the dance floor and away from the orchestra; in the centre, some green-painted tables and wooden benches forming the café of the dance hall.

Ludovic Halévy, a great friend of Degas, gives us a lifelike sketch of the Boule Noire:

> They went up the fifteen steps of the staircase and entered a vast hall in which the scents of tobacco pipes and hot wine were powerfully mingled. The orchestra, with a deafening clamour of brass, was playing a quadrille. The girls and maidservants of the *quartier* were dancing in the middle of the room. On either side of the circular promenade that ringed the dance floor, men and women were sitting at tables. You could hear the gurgle of the rough, dark red wine being poured out into white china bowls and the crunch of sugar lumps crushed into the wine with pewter spoons.

Although Baudelaire, in his piece on Constantin Guys, makes no specific reference to the haunts of pleasure in Montmartre, what he has to say about the *bals publics* applies equally well to those of Montmartre as to the ones on the left bank which he frequented. This cult of popular entertainment, the taste for prostitution that stemmed from Baudelaire, contributed largely to the success of Montmartre. To understand the power of a district henceforward devoted to pleasure over the most sensitive and over the coarsest spirits alike, one must quote the following passage:

> Women who have exaggerated fashion to the point of spoiling its grace and destroying its intention, sweep the floors ostentatiously with the trains of their dresses and the ends of their shawls; they come and go, moving back and forth, with eyes wide and startled like eyes of animals, seeming to see nothing, but watching everything. Against a background of a hellish light or against the background of an aurora borealis, red, orange, sulphur yellow, pink (pink introducing an idea of ecstasy amid the frivolity), sometimes violet (colour beloved of deaconesses, dying embers behind a blue curtain), against these magical backgrounds, with their various effects of Bengal light, there springs up the variegated image of a dubious beauty. Here majestic, there delicate, now slim, even frail, and now gigantic; now small and sparkling, now heavy and monumental. It is a good picture of the savagery inside civilization. It has its own beauty, which comes from Evil, always devoid of spirituality but now and then touched with a weariness that seems like melancholy.

6
THE COMMUNE

The new eighteenth *arrondissement* included districts scattered over the slopes of Montmartre which had not previously formed part of the old parish. They were poor districts, some working-class, others dedicated to vice, especially to the east, about the remains of the Château Rouge, an eighteenth-century summer house, brick-built, its gardens cut up and the house itself turned into a dance hall frequented by prostitutes and their protectors. In these districts, neglected by the imperial government, they did not have 'the right ideas'. Consequently, Montmartre elected as its mayor a republican doctor, Georges Clemenceau, a brilliant, cultured person with an artistic taste rare in one of his background, but still driven by hatred and later involved in compromising parliamentary scandals. Although his energy had much to do with the victory of 1918, his prejudices were an even greater factor in establishing a deplorable peace. Clemenceau was just the mayor for this turbulent commune.

During the siege of 1870–1, the ballroom of the Elysée-Montmartre was turned into a factory for the manufacture of the balloons which enabled the people of Paris to maintain contact with the rest of France. In one of these balloons, a lawyer from the south named Gambetta departed from the summit of the Butte to join the provisional government in Bordeaux and urge it to continue the already disastrous war with Prussia. Here again, Montmartre saw itself as the incarnation of resistance. When the Germans entered Paris, on 1 March 1871, Clemenceau tried, too late, to preach calm to his commune. Humiliation, the miseries endured during the siege and violent revolutionary propaganda all combined to fan the first sparks of the Commune upon the hill of Montmartre. The Commune may even be said to have been born on Montmartre, for it was here that the national guards rebelled openly against the troops of the government set up at Versailles, which was too reactionary for their liking and bent on restoring France to order as quickly as possible after the invasion. On 11 March, those national guards who supported the insurrection seized the guns belonging to a regiment of regulars and carried them up to the top of the Butte with the object of firing on the troops who were trying to keep order in Paris. The same had happened after the capture of the Bastille; but this time things rapidly worsened.

There are photographs showing the site on which the Sacré-Cœur was to be built transformed into an artillery park and bivouacs at the foot of the chalky cliffs lined with buildings already falling into disrepair and houses still countrified in appearance. The government's decision to take back those seventy-one guns decided the Commune. Two generals, Lecomte and Clément-Thomas, with such loyal troops as remained to them, attempted to recapture the guns. After a skirmish in the Boulevard de Clichy, the two generals were taken prisoner and led away, amid the jeers of the populace, to the Château Rouge, where a kind of rebel headquarters had been set up. Clemenceau, seeing that things were getting out of hand, cried out: 'No bloodshed, my friends, no bloodshed!' But to no avail. The generals were dragged out into a garden in the Rue des Rosiers, then they were shot and their bodies thrown into the common grave in the cemetery of St Vincent.

Manet: *Clemenceau* (detail), 1879–80. Paris, Louvre

Thus Montmartre had taken the lead in all the madness of the Commune. The cabarets became political clubs. There was the Club de la Revolution at the Elysée-Montmartre, the Club de la Vengeance at the Reine Blanche. Anyone might speak and the most outrageous motions were passed. The women's club at the Boule Noire in the Boulevard de Rochechouart drew crowds to listen to Louise Michel. She was a working woman, swarthy-skinned and ugly, who was distinguished among the hysterical concierges by a great talent for oratory, a kind of incantatory power. People came from all over Paris to hear her. Until the middle of May, the Commune kept its hold on Paris, the representatives of Montmartre were notable for their extremism and the population erected barricades in the streets going up to the Butte, to turn it into a fortress ready to resist the threat of attack by government troops. In the last week in May, the communards did in fact try to reform themselves in Montmartre and offer a last desperate resistance to the troops from Versailles that were advancing on Paris. But their strength was too scattered for any concerted action. Then hordes of women rushed down from the Butte to set fire to the

Gambetta leaving in a balloon during the Seige of Paris, 1870

(*above*) The shot Communards being buried in the Montmartre cemetery on 25 May 1871

(*below*) The execution of General Lecomte and General Thomas by the Communards on 18 March 1871

The fair on the Boulevard de Clichy and the Taverne du Bagne

Tuileries, the Palais-Royal and the Hôtel de Ville, and not forgetting the house of Monsieur Thiers in the Place Saint-Georges. For three nights the black outline of Montmartre loomed over a blazing Paris.

On the last day, Montmartre fell to the government troops and many of its inhabitants, fleeing eastwards, were cut down in the cemetery of Père Lachaise. But there was more firing still in the cemetery of Montmartre, a real manhunt amongst the graves. Afterwards, the bodies were piled into a single trench. And so the blood of the martyred communards made Montmartre quite as sacred to the revolutionaries as the blood of the Christian martyrs had done to the citizens of Paris in the middle ages.

Once the terror was past, the heroines of the Commune struck impressionable minds as beings worthy to inspire the Marquis de Sade. One such was Judith, the beautiful incendiary, the mistress of the journalist Victor Noir, who was murdered by a cousin of Napoleon III: 'A tall, dark girl with the face of a maenad, her eyes oozing sensuality, her powerful forehead helmeted with a thick, wild mane of hair, breasts jutting forward under her bodice' (Jean Lorrain). The hunt for those communards who had escaped the firing squad or the convict chain went on for several years. Sometimes they would be picked up in the dance halls of Montmartre, having become pimps or joined up with gangs of thieves.

As soon as the communards were out of prison, by about 1885, many of them naturally found their way back to Montmartre. One of the most picturesque was a

The Taverne du Bagne, about 1890. The waiters are dressed as convicts and the cashier as a jailer

Captain Maxime Lisbonne, who, endowed with all the prestige of the Commune, used to draw the public into various cabarets. He began with the Taverne du Bagne, a hut in a piece of waste ground with the waiters dressed as convicts and the walls daubed with pictures representing episodes of the Commune. After that he had the Brasserie des Frites Revolutionnaires and finally the Casino des Concierges. Each time there was an election, Lisbonne would stand and plaster his anarchist programme all over the walls of the eighteenth *arrondissement*. And so the spirit of revolt, smothered for nearly twenty years, was able to offer an ideal to people who would otherwise have been nothing but common murderers. And amongst the anarchists were some even more visionary. They were numerous in the bohemian literary world and most of their newspapers were printed in Montmartre. The audiences who applauded Bruant's songs at the Chat Noir inclined to them, although admittedly more out of a kind of snobbery than because they understood their wretchedness or had any thoughts of relieving it. The anarchists and their girls became in the end just one amongst the erotic fantasies of the *fin de siècle*. Memories of the Commune would crop up again in numerous songs sung by girls in black dresses with red scarves round their necks, the *goualeuses*. Jacques Becker's film, *Casque d'Or*, made in 1955 with Simone Signoret as the dancer at the Moulin Rouge who is the mistress of an anarchist, was a splendid evocation of the dramatic and poetic atmosphere of this Montmartre, born of the Commune.

7
THE SACRÉ~COEUR

Refuge of unappreciated artists, haunt of pleasure-seekers and finally cradle of the Commune, from 1871 onwards Montmartre had become the symbol of everything most shocking to the bourgeois. But a comparatively recent cult restored to the Mons Martyrum all its old prestige. The worship of the Sacred Heart of Jesus had been initiated in 1689 by a Burgundian nun, St Marguerite-Marie Alacoque, and achieved a good deal of popularity with female congregations, especially among the Benedictines of Montmartre at the end of the seventeenth century. But it was not until the Second Empire that the cult became really popular and every Catholic home had its colour print of Christ with a flaming heart. After the defeat at Sedan, a Jesuit suggested placing France under the protection of the Sacred Heart and the chant went up from every church: 'Save Rome and France in the name of the Sacred Heart.' In fact, taking advantage of France's enfeebled state, the Italians had taken control of Rome and the Pope declared himself a prisoner in the Vatican. After the defeat and the Commune the Catholics decided to build a church in Paris in expiation, dedicated to the Sacred Heart, which should be entreated to bring about the liberation of the papacy (which came about in 1929) and the return of Alsace to France (which took place in 1918). The plan was an immediate success. Millions flowed in and the archbishop of Paris, Cardinal Guibert, decided that the basilica should be erected on Montmartre. 'It is here', the prelate cried, 'that the Sacred Heart should be enthroned, to draw all to itself, on the summit of the hill upon which Christendom was born in the blood of the first apostles, the monument to our religious rebirth should be raised.'

The Assemblée Nationale forwarded the business in 1873 by offering all the land that lay behind the church of Saint-Pierre, and was occupied by *guinguettes*, allotments and a fairground. There were instant protests. The minister of war had his eye on the site to build a fort. The archbishop answered him: 'Let me build my fortress, it will be well worth yours.' The republicans, with little representation in the assembly but backed by the Freemasons, declared: 'The temple of superstition will dominate the capital of light!' The architect chosen was a second-rate disciple of Viollet-le-Duc, Paul Abadie, who had done some very bad restoration on the cathedrals of Périgueux and Angoulême. Yet the choice was a wise one. Inspired by Saint-Front at Périgueux, Abadie conceived a somewhat Byzantine church with domes and pinnacles, flanked by a campanile. And it must be admitted that Abadie's somewhat oriental silhouette crowns the Butte far better than the Neo-Classical temple once dreamed of by Napoleon or the Neo-Gothic plans preferred by the archbishop would ever have done.

The actual building did not go altogether smoothly. It was necessary to dig gigantic foundations, to shore up ground undermined by the quarries. Hardly was the crypt completed before funds ran out. For more than thirty years the clergy, with remarkable ingenuity, extracted from the faithful the sums needed to finish the building. Anyone who gave the cost of a stone could have his name carved on it,

Rue de l'Abreuvoir and the Sacré-Cœur. Photo Desoye

Utrillo: *Renoir's garden* (detail), 1879–80. New York, Mr Grégoire Tarnopol

A procession round the Sacré-Cœur before its completion, about 1890

wealthy parishes, distinguished families gave columns, statues, mosaics and even whole chapels. Savoy made a gift of a huge bell, which was ceremoniously christened the Savoyarde. The Sacré-Cœur was truly built by that patriotic, working-class Catholic France which so exasperated the intellectuals. Standing under those arches decorated with second-rate mosaics and reading all those simple ex-votos, one might be wading through the monotonous litany of a poem by Péguy. Not one single artist of distinction contributed to the decoration of this monument. When the republicans came to power there were redoubled attacks upon the shrine, which was rising painfully from the earth and was already beginning to look like a provocation. A good speech by the Marquis de Mun in the Chamber of Deputies in 1897 just saved the Sacré-Cœur. But the money was still flowing in. Pilgrimages were arranged as soon as it was possible to say mass in the crypt. On 2 August 1914 the last step of the stairs up to the campanile was put in place.

Infuriated by this success, the anti-clericals had unearthed a Chevalier de la Barre who had been put to death by Louis XV for insulting a procession, and erected a statue to him at the foot of the basilica. This affront only heightened the zeal of the faithful. The Germans melted the statue down in 1943 and it has never been replaced. To the anarchists, the Sacré-Cœur, built at a cost of millions of francs, represented the triumph of the capitalist Church. When Steinlen designed the poster for the launching of the paper *Le Petit Sou*, he depicted the Sacré-Cœur with a golden calf in its doorway being threatened by Liberty, swathed in red.

The war gave a fresh impetus to the generosity of the French people, whose need of the help of the Sacred Heart was greater than it had ever been. And victory justified their faith. On 16 October 1919, the basilica was consecrated in the presence of nine cardinals, twelve archbishops and ninety bishops, and in their midst the legate charged with the blessings of Benedict XV. There have been no apparitions to draw the crowds or miracles to revive their fervour, yet the basilica is still visited at least as much by worshippers as by the tourists who go there to admire the view from its portico, which is a favourite haunt of hippies. A community of Benedictines sees to the smooth running of the shrine which has restored Montmartre to its role as a sacred hill.

But although literary and artistic Montmartre stood very much aloof from the building of the Sacré-Cœur, the outline of the basilica had no sooner begun to dominate the Butte than it was inspiring poets and painters. Moreover the thought of those Byzantine domes lording it over the capital delighted the supporters of a Catholic revival. One such, Léon Bloy, lived for a long time, bitter and impoverished, in the shadow of the Sacré-Cœur while it was still in building, without ever receiving that grace which is the forgiveness of sins. Having made his début in the cabaret of the Chat Noir he had there learned the art of invective and a contempt for all things bourgeois. Henry Miller, on the other hand, who, much later, about 1930, lived in the Place Clichy, was once touched with grace before the Sacré-Cœur.

8
THE MOULIN DE LA GALETTE

Impressionism is first and foremost a right-bank school, lying as far as possible from the Ecole des Beaux-Arts; it is even the school of one particular area of the right bank dominated by Montmartre. The Impressionists' *quartier* went from the Gare Saint-Lazare to the Opéra, barely overstepping the *grands boulevards*. The Rue Laffitte and its picture dealers were one of its centres, as were the Quartier de l'Europe, where Mallarmé lived, and the Batignolles, criss-crossed by railway lines, where Zola lodged in his early days. Clichy, more working class, and above all Montmartre provided a home for most of the Impressionists at one time or another. Outside this capital, comprising the better part of two *arrondissements*, was a kind of garden suburb, Bougival, Chatou. . . .

Montmartre in 1874 still had some of the charm of those outlying districts, but above the gardens the new buildings were visible, as they are in Sisley's picture, and at the bottom of the Butte to the north were factory chimneys and gasometers. For the first time, a great school of painting flourished in a mediocre setting, at its best picturesque, with little gardens and summer houses such as Guillaumin was painting in 1865. There was no need of an impressive architectural background as in Rome or Venice, of great urban refinement as in Florence, of bourgeois dignity as in Holland, or of a romantic landscape as was the case with the recent English painters and the masters of Barbizon. The palaces which the new school frequented were those of the common people, almost of the dregs of society, like the Moulin de la Galette; the streets they painted were the most commonplace; their Capitol was the Gare Saint-Lazare. There were reasons for their choice, both conscious and unconscious. Amongst the former was the heritage of Naturalism, distaste for an aesthetic based on an accepted idea of Beauty as it was taught at the Ecole des Beaux-Arts. The young painters, not one of whom had ever been to Rome, declared that their *quartier* was quite as worthy to be painted as the banks of the Tiber. But there were deeper reasons driving painters who rejected official teaching to seek inspiration in the ordinary, the urge to democracy – not that they had any very clearly defined political ideas, but they felt that truth was no longer in temples and palaces, that the people, as Zola was beginning to depict them in his novels, represented the greatest social value. That Zola gave such encouragement to the Impressionists was not because they exemplified his aesthetic ideal but because, like him, they rejected official humanism.

It is significant that a party to celebrate the success of *L'Assommoir* should have been held at the Elysée-Montmartre. It was a great occasion and all the guests belonging to literary and theatrical society were to go dressed as artisans or street girls. (*L'Assommoir* is the story of an alcoholic artisan from Belleville, not far from Montmartre, and his daughter is Nana, the great courtesan.) At that time the section of the lower classes from which prostitutes and petty thieves were recruited, what Marx called the *Lumpenproletariat* and which is called the *populo* in France, occupied in the bourgeois imagination (only painted black rather than white) the

The old entrance to the Moulin de la Galette, about 1890

The Bal de l'Assommoir. Drawing by Daniel Vierge in *Le Monde Illustré*

place held by shepherds in the aristocratic imaginations of the previous century. This interest continued to grow, whence a whole body of literature which gave society readers a delicious thrill by depicting the adventures of pimps and the prostitutes who worked for them.

But this is to digress. The Impressionists were delightful people who had nothing to do with the riff-raff. Their models, who frequently became their mistresses for a season or two, or even for life, like Madame Renoir, were the daughters of the romantic Mimi Pinson or country girls come to work in Paris. Renoir settled on the outskirts of Montmartre soon after his arrival in Paris and remained there for nearly forty years. In the early years he was to be found in the Rue Cortot and the Rue Tourlaque; for a time he had a studio in the Bateau-Lavoir in the Place Ravignan, and he settled finally at the Château des Brouillards, a building standing in a wild garden, in a summer house from which he overlooked the whole suburb to the north. Cézanne had a studio in the Rue Hégésippe Moreau, although not for very long. Camille Pissarro lived successively in the Rue des Trois Frères and the Rue de

The Bal de l'Assommoir. Zola alone wears tails amongst artists dressed as characters from his novel

l'Abreuvoir. A great English writer who at one time saw himself as a painter, George Moore, has left a description of a walk in Montmartre which is a real guide book to the Impressionists, every sentence is a subject for a painting.

Today I drive to breakfast through the white torridities of the Rue Blanche seeing the back of the coachman growing drowsier; it would have rounded off into sleep long ago had it not been for the great paving stones that swing the vehicle from side to side in the Rue Blanche; and feeling that the poor fainting animal will not be able to climb the Rue Lepic to draw me to the Butte, I dismiss the carriage, half out of pity, and a wish to study the Rue Lepic, so typical it is of the upper lower classes. In the Rue Blanche there are *porte-cochères* but in the Rue Lepic the narrow doors, partially grated, open on narrow passages at the end of which, squeezed between the wall and the stairs are small rooms where concierges sit, *en camisole*, peeling vegetables and sewing. The wooden blinds flung back on faded yellow walls reveal a strip of white bed curtain and a heavy,

Zola's tomb

The Maquis near the Moulin de la Galette, about 1890

middle-aged woman looking into a cupboard in which a rabbit lies sleeping; her man, a cobbler, sits hammering in the window, and the smell of leather follows the passenger for several steps. A few doors up the street a girl sits trimming her bonnet. The girl is pale with the exhausting heat. At the corner of the next street there is a Marchand de vin. Opposite, a dirty little *charbonnier* stands in front of a little hole which he calls his *boutique*. A group of women in discoloured *peignoirs* and heavy carpet slippers go by with baskets in their arms. Everywhere traces of meagre and humble life, but nowhere the demented wretch so common in our London streets. . . . At the top of the street I enter a still poorer neighbourhood, a still steeper street but so narrow that a thin line of shadow has already begun to appear on the pavement. At the top of the street is a stairway, and above the stairway a grassy knoll, and above the knoll a windmill lifts its black and motionless arms. For the mill is now a mute ornament, a sign for the Bal du Moulin de la Galette. . . . As the street ascends it grows whiter, some bygone architecture attracts my attention, a dilapidated façade and broken pillars; and standing in the midst of ruined gardens, circled by high walls, crumbling and white, and looking through a broken gateway I see a fountain splashing.

Nearly every Saturday, Renoir would go dancing at the Moulin de la Galette with two painter friends, Georges Rivière and Goeneutte. There he danced happily with pretty girls. When he determined to capture these happy times in a monumental canvas painted on the spot (*see opposite p. 31*), Renoir took the advice of his friend Georges Rivière and looked for a lodging near the Moulin.

As soon as Renoir crossed the threshold, he was delighted with the sight of the garden, which looked like a beautiful, neglected park. Passing through the narrow hall of the little house, one found oneself facing a huge lawn of unmown grass dotted with poppies, convolvulus and daisies. Beyond that, a fine avenue of mature trees and beyond that again an orchard and vegetable garden, then a shrubbery. . . . He rented two enormous rooms and a stable to store his canvases in. . . . Thus our days were spent happily between the old lodging in the Rue Cortot and the Moulin, where Renoir worked in the afternoons at his great canvas of the Ball. We carried this canvas from the Rue Cortot to the Moulin every day because the picture was painted entirely on the spot. This was not always very easy going when there was a wind blowing and the big stretcher threatened to fly away like a kite above the Butte.

There is a record of the names of the dancers of the Moulin de la Galette who posed for Renoir. Estelle is on the bench in the foreground, Margot is in the middle dancing with a Cuban painter. Some friends, Rivière, Lestringuey and Gervex, are sitting on café chairs at the wooden table, drinking from tall glasses. It can be seen that the

furniture has remained rustic; only the great gas chandeliers between the trees could lend a touch of tawdry glamour. Who would have believed that three years earlier those same chandeliers had illuminated the meetings of the communards in the grim month of May 1871? Even when he was discovering Italy, Renoir was still nostalgic for the Moulin de la Galette. 'I am a little dull away from Montmartre, the least *grisette* is worth more than the loveliest Neapolitan girl,' he wrote to a friend.

Was it at the Moulin de la Galette that, in 1884 or thereabouts, Renoir met a lovely dark girl with slanting eyes called Suzanne Valadon? She, at all events, was fond of telling how, after she had posed for him for the *Danse à la Campagne*, Renoir wanted to sleep with her. Madame Renoir apparently put an end to that affair with a broomstick. Out of spite, she never referred to Renoir except as the 'tomato sauce painter', probably alluding to the reddish tint he used liberally in rather too many of his later paintings. This is our first encounter with this formidable woman, but we shall be meeting her again because she made news in Montmartre for fifty years.

If the fashion for the Moulin de la Galette had its literary origin in Zola's novels, Renoir borrowed nothing from the writer beyond a wish to portray his time, a feeling for light and for youthful flesh; happily he had no social message. No picture is more a young man's picture, full of the joys of life, turning a commonplace setting and some nice but vulgar girls into a kind of Cythera of the people, a descendant of the aristocratic Cythera of Watteau. From then on youth and vulgarity were part of the myth of Montmartre.

For a long time the Moulin de la Galette remained a respectable place with none of the shocking or expensive attractions with which newer establishments were drawing a richer and more mixed clientele. In 1895, for instance, there was this account to be read in the *Pick Me Up*:

They dance little steps nobody ever saw before on land or sea. They mimic the great people with their airs and graces. They try and kick like the 'great dancers' of whom they have 'heard tell'. They give vent to all the quips and pranks of their ill-bred little fancies, and stunted little dreams, and it's good, very good, to see. . . . The boys are roughs, the gamin grown up, with his tongue in the side of his cheek, and his old-world shrewdness, and the sharpness which fighting against starvation has put into his eyes and into the hard lines about his lips. And their sweethearts! The sweethearts are all belles, no wallflowers here. They are frank and honest to a degree in their methods. If they want a man to dance they ask him. . . . They gambol, and prank, and joke, and guy one another. They play 'tag', and between the dances race after each other over and under the chairs and tables; and the proprietor, M. Pouillaude, looks on indulgently and smiles, and the policeman at the door yawns, with mirth in his eyes and the memory of 'when he made an ass of himself too', and one or two old men onlookers recount audibly their belief that 'youth is, after all, the best thing in the world'.

Renoir: *Under the arbour at the Moulin de la Galette*, 1876. Moscow, Pushkin Museum

9
THE NOUVELLE ATHÈNES

If the Moulin de la Galette was the subject of one of the great Impressionist pictures and the place of entertainment of the young painters, the intellectual centre of Impressionism was lower down, at the café of the Nouvelle Athènes, on the corner of the Place Pigalle. The fashion for this establishment superseded that of the Café Guerbois in the Avenue de Clichy, where the young painters used to meet during the Second Empire, often with Zola, more rarely Mallarmé, in their midst. These two writers put in only brief appearances at the Nouvelle Athènes. Literature was represented there by Villiers de l'Isle Adam, ever ready to tell strange tales to anyone who would buy him a drink, sometimes by Verlaine and frequently by Catulle Mendès. The critic Duranty was also to be seen there. Manet would come in, prim and affable, to be immediately surrounded by young painters. Degas, who lived only a step or two away, in the Rue Victor Massé, preferred a smaller circle, one better able to appreciate the wit of his conversation. There were days when Degas did not even bow to Manet.

This café was a veritable school of aesthetics for many young men, like George Moore, who felt that there was nothing further to be gained from Oxford:

> I can hear the glass door of the café grate on the sands as I open it. I can recall the smell of every hour. In the morning that of eggs frizzling in butter, the pungent cigarette, coffee and bad cognac; at five o'clock the fragrant odour of absinthe; soon after, the steaming soup ascends from the kitchen; and as the evening advances, the mingled smell of cigarettes, coffee and weak beer. A partition rising a few feet or more over the hats separates the glass front from the main body of the café. The usual marble tables are there, and it is there we sat and aestheticised till two o'clock in the morning.

What Oxford don would have had the pernicious charm of Catulle Mendès, the Parnassian poet:

> Catulle Mendès, a perfect realisation of his name with his pale hair, his fragile face illuminated with the idealism of a depraved woman. He takes you by the arm, by the hand, he leans towards you, his words are caresses, his fervour is delightful, and to hear him is like to drink a smooth, perfumed yellow wine.

Touched by Moore's eagerness, Manet did a watercolour of him (*see page 136*) at the Nouvelle Athènes. Pale and ingenuous, the young man, like all Manet's models, has an expression revealing no curiosity, not the least metaphysical concern, merely a slight boredom. In the eyes of the *demi-mondaines*, Irma Blumer or Nina de Callias, who dropped in from time to time to find relief among the painters from the boredom of their wealthy lovers, Manet seems to read nothing but a purely animal pleasure. Women aroused in him the same degree of interest as a bunch of flowers, no more. Cézanne must have gone to the Nouvelle Athènes sometimes during his increasingly infrequent visits to Paris, but he could have repeated what he said when

Degas: *Edmond Duranty*, 1879. Glasgow Art Gallery (Burrell Collection loan)

(*overleaf*) Degas: Women on the terrace, about 1877. Paris, Louvre

Self-portrait by Suzanne Valadon

Pissarro took him to the Café Guerbois for the first time, on seeing painters so far from bohemian: 'The damn fellows are as well-dressed as lawyers.' That would certainly have applied to Manet, always impeccably turned out, and even to Degas who, in spite of a certain carelessness, possibly an affectation, did not forget that he had been a dandy when he went up to Montmartre. At the Nouvelle Athènes, Manet, Degas and Alfred Stevens were gentlemen. The courteous Manet and the caustic Degas took little pleasure in each other's society. Nor should it be thought that this café was a kind of club, like some romantic cafés, or a forum where everyone had to go, as the Coupole in Montparnasse was to become. No, it was a place to drop into, where one could usually come across a friend or two. People went there more to pick holes in the latest Salon successes than to evolve great theories of art.

An Italian had established what amounted to a real market for artists' models at the *rond-point* of the Place Pigalle, not at all the well-built Italians the members of the Institut liked to draw, but strange girls of all ages for, as Francis Carco truly said, in Montmartre, in 1880 or so, they preferred character to beauty. Degas met Puvis de Chavannes there. The academic masters chose their Venuses there, their Blanches de Castille, their *Amour mutin* or *Ange consolateur*. Degas would murmur as the solemn Puvis passed by: 'What a bore!' Was it in this model market or in one of the dancing schools that trained concierges' daughters for the Opéra, that Degas found the fourteen-year-old girl who, in 1881, in a studio at 19 bis Rue Fontaine, posed for a sculpture in wax (long afterwards cast in bronze)? Certainly it was a true daughter of Montmartre who inspired his lines:

> *Si Montmartre a donné l'esprit et les aïeux,*
> *Roxelane le nez et la Chine les yeux,*
> *Attentif Ariel donne à cette recrue*
> *Tes pas légers de jours, tes pas légers de nuit;*
> *Fais que, pour mon plaisir, elle sente son fruit*
> *Et garde, au palais d'or, la race de sa rue.*

> If Montmartre gave her wits and ancestry,
> Roxelana's nose and China's eyes,
> So, careful Ariel, give this new recruit
> Thy light step by day, thy light step by night;
> And let her keep her own rich scent for my delight,
> And in the golden halls retain the breeding of her street.

Alas, the saucy dancer, with her kittenish face, was, almost certainly, going to become one of those beribboned hags whom Degas had drawn on the terrace of the Nouvelle Athènes in 1875, or even, with the years, raddled by absinth, like that Ellen Andrée, painted beside Desboutin (*see opposite p. 86*). Marcelin Desboutin, excellent engraver and still better talker, full of theories, paradoxes and invective, spent the better part of his time at the Nouvelle Athènes. An incorrigible bohemian who had led a colourful life in Italy, he, like Villiers de l'Isle Adam, found in Montmartre an audience to listen to him and buy him drinks. Another customer of the Nouvelle Athènes who crossed over from the model market to the café terrace was Suzanne Valadon. Degas took up the clever, vicious girl. He would talk painting to her as he painted. She started drawing and Degas was attracted by her firm, rather studiedly masculine line. Puvis de Chavannes, for whom she also posed, taught her to hold a brush and, she said, got her with child. There was a good deal of talk about Suzanne Valadon at the Nouvelle Athènes.

N. Goeneutte: *Boulevard de Clichy under snow*, 1876. London, Tate Gallery

Degas was particularly admired by two young painters who were accidentally enrolled among the Impressionists as a result of an exhibition: Boldini and Forain. The first of these painted with the incredible precision of a Meissonier, but an enervated Meissonier who would suddenly distort women and perspective in a kind of erotic frenzy. In his youthful canvases, in which we find the qualities of Meissonier and the eye of Degas, Boldini has left many views of Montmartre in the eighties, the Place Clichy with a whole host of omnibuses, fiacres and handcarts coming and going round the monument to the Defence of 1814. This lecherous little man depicted studios that were more like bachelor apartments: divans, bearskins, innumerable cushions, green plants and shaded lamps, all treated with a nervous precision. We owe to him, too, a view of the Place Pigalle as seen from the Café de la Nouvelle Athènes.

Forain, on the other hand, painted the interior of the café, the stupid, avaricious women of the type established by Degas. Forain was only an occasional denizen of Montmartre. His celebrated wit, with its basis of cynicism and anti-Semitism, belonged to a more Parisian Paris. Forain did not often draw characters from Montmartre but he was involved in one episode of literary history, the first of any importance to take place on the slopes of Montmartre, the meeting, in 1872, of Verlaine and Rimbaud.

Zola, in one of his lesser novels, *L'Oeuvre*, has described the life of the regulars of the Nouvelle Athènes. The hero, Claude Lantier, contains much less of Cézanne than is generally supposed; his style may be Impressionist but his inspiration is rather realist. 'He went, in the snows of December, to stand for four hours every day facing the Butte Montmartre, at the corner of a piece of waste ground from where he painted a wretched background of low hovels with factory chimneys looming over them, while in the foreground, in the snow, he had put a small girl and a ragged urchin guzzling stolen apples.'

Friends on the make or failures, possessive women who ultimately cared little for their lovers' talent, that is the artistic world of the Butte as it was during the last third of the century. Poverty, a little drink and endless talk. In the end, Lantier hangs himself in his studio in the Rue Tourlaque and makes one more burial at the church of Saint-Pierre:

> Slowly the hearse climbed the steep slope, the end of which rounded the side of the Butte Montmartre; now and then side streets plunged abruptly downwards, offering glimpses of the vastness of Paris, wide and deep as a sea. When they came out in front of the church of Saint-Pierre and carried the coffin up, it hung there for an instant above the great city. Under that grey, wintry sky, with great clouds flying, driven on the breath of an icy wind, the city looked larger, unending, in the rolling haze that thickened menacingly on the horizon. The pitiful corpse, who had meant to conquer it, passed before it on its way back to the earth.

10
CHEZ LE PÈRE TANGUY

During the Second Empire, the picture dealers had luxuriously appointed galleries off the *grands boulevards*, not far from the Bourse: damasks and house plants, amongst which their wealthy customers selected works whose authors were familiar to them from their successes at the Salon. There was nothing like that in Montmartre. It was either junk shops or paint shops which would be willing to hang the works of young artists on their walls. The former covered the pavement with old iron, second-hand furniture and used canvases which penniless young painters would buy to paint over. And inside the shop, amid the jumble that was often carefully arranged to give the customer the illusion of a discovery, were daubs black with age and young men's work. It was common to see respectable bourgeois emerging from these shops with a furtive air, a badly wrapped package under their arms; they had been indulging in a secret passion for the works of young painters, which they would then stow away in cupboards, safe from the outcry of their families. One of these second-hand dealers, Père Martin, bought a Renoir, *La Loge*, for 485 francs, the amount of the rent that was owing. Long afterwards, in conversation with a great dealer, Ambroise Vollard, who had himself done some good business by rummaging in Montmartre, Renoir recalled those dealers:

> Besides Père Martin, there was another dealer in Montmartre who sold very fine pictures. But surely, Vollard, you must have known Portier? What a funny way he had, that one, of puffing up his wares. 'Don't buy that picture! It's much too dear!' The customer would generally buy it. Admittedly what was called dear, even in 1895, was paying two thousand francs for a first class Manet. Portier had a basement in the Rue Lepic, Père Martin a ground floor at the bottom of the Rue des Martyrs; they were shabby but what magnificent pictures were to be seen there! The whole Impressionist school, not to mention the Corots and Delacroixs and Daumiers and I don't know what!

The paint sellers had smarter shops and the painters liked to linger there for a chat. The shopkeepers would often take canvases in lieu of payment; most famous of them was Père Tanguy and his fame was due as much to Van Gogh's portrait (*see opposite p. 87*) as to his own talent and generosity. A Breton by birth and as stubborn and nonconformist as all his countrymen, Tanguy had come to Paris in about 1860. He worked as a colour mixer for Edouard, who supplied all the best artists, then began making his own for some young painters with whom he struck up an acquaintance, including Monet and Cézanne. He was compromised during the Commune and imprisoned and did not return until 1874, when he opened a small shop. He was always willing to help young artists and to find buyers for them. Tanguy was particularly fond of Cézanne, in whom he found something of his own obstinacy and disinterestedness. He sometimes had as many as thirty Cézannes in his storeroom and did not mind that he rarely sold one, and never for more than forty francs. He would show the canvases of the master of Aix religiously, whether to young artists or

Junk shop in the Maquis run by the poet Dalechamps

Félix Fénéon outside La Goulue's booth. Painting by Toulouse-Lautrec, 1895. Paris, Louvre

to older masters who were intrigued by the legend of Cézanne, to which Zola had contributed, for was he not (although I have already voiced my own doubts) the Lantier of *L'Oeuvre*? Ambroise Vollard explains very well the influence that Père Tanguy was able to exercise over young painters:

'To belong to the School' was, for him, the same thing as that other quality: 'to be modern'; and to encompass such an end, according to Père Tanguy, it was necessary, first and foremost, to banish the 'tobacco juice' from one's palette and 'paint thick'. Anyone who had the nerve to ask for a tube of black was therefore unpopular in his house, although in the end, out of the goodness of his heart, Père Tanguy would reinstate the unfortunate painter who was trying to gain an

honest living with ivory black. What was more, like the bourgeois for whom he professed such scorn, the worthy Tanguy was, in his heart of hearts, convinced that hard work and good behaviour were not merely necessary conditions but the certain secret of success.

One of Père Tanguy's most constant visitors was Paul Signac, himself a child of the Butte, who had learned to paint in the free studio (you went when you liked and paid a moderate sum) of a former winner of the Prix de Rome, Bin, now mayor of Montmartre. For his landscapes, he was long content with painting the waste areas of Clichy. Signac had two great friends, the Symbolist landscape painter Henri Rivière, who designed the shadow plays at the Chat Noir, and Seurat. Much more intellectual than the Impressionists, whom they admired, these young men evolved a new theory, called Divisionism, and became involved with Symbolist critics, some of them with anarchist leanings, like Félix Fénéon. Fénéon, the best critic of a modern style of painting, contributor to the *Chat Noir* and later to the *Revue Blanche*, was a familiar figure in Tanguy's little shop. His articles were always the first to herald painters who were transcending outworn formulae, however new they were. Anquetin and Emile Bernard were both encouraged while they were bringing something new to painting. Fénéon's great friend was Maximilien Luce and the two of them were involved in the anarchist trials of 1894. He wrote of Luce, as early as 1888:

From Montmartre, the panorama of Paris stretches out, rolling on for kilometres without M. Luce ever resorting to the primitive subterfuge of towers and domes of decreasing height spaced out at intervals to indicate perspective; a broad ray of sunshine falls obliquely through the piled up clouds, polychroming them, and dusts the farther reaches of the city.

(*Le Néo-Impressionisme aux Indépendants*)

The arrival of a new Gauguin was an event to be communicated to the little reviews. Thin and desiccated, with a goatee beard and a hooked nose like the late President Lincoln, Fénéon was such a characteristic figure on the Butte that Toulouse-Lautrec, another friend of his, painted him outside the booth of La Goulue. Fénéon's admiration for Seurat is well known. But the latter was so solitary, so wrapped up in his studies, so completely indifferent, that one hesitates to mention him amongst those who contributed to the myth of Montmartre, and yet he too was inspired by the fairground booths erected in the Boulevard Rochechouart for one of his biggest pictures and the *Poseuses* are artists' models from Montmartre. Seurat died in a hotel in the Passage de l'Elysée des Beaux-Arts and, in his last days, he expressed a wish to paint a view of it from the top of the Place Clichy which should be as important as *La Grande Jatte*. Fénéon and Signac found several Seurats in Père Tanguy's back shop when they were helping his widow to clear it in 1894. The Cézannes were sent to the sale room, where they made very little. A committee, including Rodin and Puvis

Picasso's portrait of Clovis Sagot, the clown who became a picture dealer

Berthe Weill, the picture dealer, by Picasso

de Chavannes, was formed to rescue Mère Tanguy from poverty. This shows how highly they all thought of the old *marchand de couleurs*.

Signac was the most active and the most keenly intellectual of the Post-Impressionists; his studio in the Boulevard de Clichy was open to painters and writers alike. Maximilien Luce, Charles Cross and Van Gogh were all to be seen there in 1887. Signac certainly converted Van Gogh to a lighter style of painting, using clear, unmixed colours. They met at Père Tanguy's, whose acquaintance Van Gogh had probably made on his first, brief stay in Paris, from May 1875 to March 1876. He wrote to his brother Theo on 6 July 1875: 'I have a little room in Montmartre which you would like; it is small but looks on to a little garden carpeted with ivy and a vine.' And Van Gogh drew the view from his room. He also painted the belvedere in the Place du Tertre, a *guinguette*, the Bonne Franquette at 18 Rue des Saules, and a view of the heath. The influence of Raffaelli, a local painter dear to Degas, is clear at this time. There is something delicate and picturesque there, with the acid colours that mark the work of this self-taught painter, then much prized and regarded as 'modern'. The burgeoning of Van Gogh, until then given to gloomy subject matter and treatment, dates from this first visit.

Ten years later, Vincent returned to Paris and took up residence first with his brother in the Rue de Laval and then at 54 Rue Lepic. He had his meals at Mère Bataille's restaurant where such dissimilar people were to be met with as the great socialist orator Jean Jaurès and the poet Catulle Mendès. He is thought at this time to have had an affair with La Segatori, the owner of the Mirliton, who had once modelled for Corot. At all events it was at that cabaret that he got to know Toulouse-Lautrec; he had met him for the first time at Cormon's studio, 104 Boulevard de Clichy, along with Anquetin and Emile Bernard. In July 1887, Père Tanguy showed one of Van Gogh's canvases and, in the following year, his portrait, wearing a Breton hat against a background of Japanese prints, and Père Tanguy's name cropped up frequently in Van Gogh's letters after he left Paris. From Arles, in the spring of 1888:

> I've been sorry, all the same, that I didn't order paints from Père Tanguy, not that there was the slightest advantage in it – far from it – but he's such a funny old fellow, and I often think of him even now. Don't forget to say hullo to him for me if you should see him, and tell him if he wants some pictures for his window, he shall have them from here, and better ones. Oh, it seems to me more and more that people are the root of everything.

Six months later:

> I don't know whether I shall be able to paint the postman as I feel him, this man is like Père Tanguy, a revolutionary, probably he is regarded as a good republican because he cordially detests the republic we are enjoying at present, and because, all in all, he has his doubts and is a little bit disenchanted with the idea of republicanism itself.

Van Gogh: *La Guinguette*, about 1886. Paris, Louvre

In January 1889, Van Gogh was present at a pastoral play in Provençal: one of the amateur actresses was an 'old peasant woman, just what Mme Tanguy would be like, with a brain of silex or gun flint, false, treacherous, mad.' This passage shows how insanity was gaining on Van Gogh's mind, for no one else has had a hard word to say about Mère Tanguy.

If Père Tanguy is remembered as a saint in the history of art, it is hard to say the same for the dealers who encouraged young artists after him. There was Berthe Weill, with a sharp nose for profit and a schoolmistressy look with her pince-nez. All that can be said is that it was thanks to her that Picasso did not starve to death and met with some more generous patrons. Greedier still, and very ignorant, was Clovis Sagot, at one time a clown with the Cirque Fernando, who claimed to have discovered Modigliani. Apollinaire, in a rare moment of indulgence, called him 'the Père Tanguy of modern painting'. He had set up shop in what had been a chemist's and would hand out the stocks of old remedies left on the shelves to ailing artists. He concealed his ruthlessness under the clowning that had once been his trade. On one occasion he arrived in Picasso's studio with a magnificent bunch of flowers. 'If you want to keep this bouquet, paint a picture of it for me.' Yet it was in his shop that Leo Stein discovered the *Jeune Fille à la Corbeille de Fleurs*. Gertrude did not like the head. 'Very well,' said Sagot, 'we'll cut it off.' But Leo decided to take the canvas as it was.

There was also Père Soulier, a paint seller who sold the canvases that painters left with him in lieu of payment. It was there in 1908 that Wilhelm Uhde discovered his first Picasso and there too, in the same year, that Picasso bought a portrait, *Woman in Red*, for five francs. 'You can paint over the canvas', the dealer told him, but he did nothing of the kind and so discovered Le Douanier Rousseau. Picasso showed the canvas to Apollinaire, who was very excited by it.

Père Tanguy's fame had gone to the junk dealers' heads. They too wanted to discover their Van Goghs and would buy, for chicken feed admittedly, anything that struck them as 'modern'. They would buy back from the rag-and-bone men the torn canvases that dissatisfied artists threw away. From the beginnings of Cubism there was quite a regular traffic between the Montmartre shops and those of the young dealers in the Faubourg Saint-Honoré.

11
THE CHAT NOIR

In 1881 there arrived from Normandy a good-looking young man with an unfortunate habit of painting his face: Jean Lorrain. He spent five years of his life in Montmartre, five years that were also the most dazzling ones for the hill whose chronicler he became. A brilliant journalist, with an eye that missed no blemish, no absurdity, but could fill with tears on seeing beauty in a picture, a profile, a gown. From his first poems, *Modernités*, this *fin-de-siècle* Petronius evoked the whole life of Montmartre: transvestites, lesbians, go-betweens, outrageous bluestockings, failed poets declining into pimps, wrestlers, part-time gigolos for either sex. Lorrain is still the best witness to the intellectual effervescence which took possession of Montmartre in the early 1880s and showed itself in a number of cabarets, the most famous of which was the Chat Noir.

The Chat Noir started modestly in the Boulevard Rochechouart and speedily moved to Stevens's old studio in the Rue de Laval (now Victor Massé). Before that there had been the *beuglants*, a kind of tavern where there were singers to listen to, some realistic or *cocardière*, others sentimental or Parisienne (*gommeuses*), and cafés where poets would recite their latest works. The cabarets had something of both; they gave a great many poets the chance to express themselves and a bourgeois public the opportunity to experience the thrill of a new and shocking world, for many of these works were very daring. The *nostalgie de la boue* so dear to the English aesthetes was born in Montmartre in the 1880s. Lorrain became friendly with Rodolphe Salis, who had just opened the most famous of these cabarets, for which Steinlen had designed the disturbing poster of a black cat, tail triumphantly erect, silhouetted against the red background of a Byzantine aureole.

The Chat Noir, the olla podrida of every style and every extravagance, of reach-me-down artistic bric-à-brac, of a whole *quartier* of artists and poets, a picaresque, Baroque museum of all the lucubrations of all the bohemians and all the drifters who had been washed up there in the space of twenty years; the most perfect bad taste alongside exquisite treasure trove; colourful statuettes and frescoes by Willette; flocks of slender, depraved nudes, pelted with roses and haloed in gold, with stuffed owls, wrought ironwork and china cats: illuminated bas-reliefs; the music of Delmet and the songs of Xanrof . . .

In one phrase Tailhade summed up the atmosphere: '*L'Assommoir* and the *Divine Comedy* put together.' Salis was a hefty, high-complexioned redhead in a tight brocade waistcoat and his curling hair and beard made him look like a Renaissance soldier of fortune. In his baritone voice, he would lavish copious insults on the customers of his establishment, handling invective with a tireless enthusiasm and giving his smart audiences the mild thrill of being treated as pimps and whores. There was no end to his familiarities: when the Prince of Wales visited the Chat Noir, Salis greeted him with a sympathetic 'And that mother of yours still as well as ever?'

Yes, Salis created a certain Montmartre; night after night he cried out:

The Chat Noir in 1888. Engraving in *l'Illustration*

Sketches of décor from a brasserie on the Place Clichy, about 1895

'Montmartre the free city, Montmartre the sacred hill, Montmartre the germ of the earth, navel and brain of the world, the granite breast at which generations in love with an ideal come to slake their thirst.' He even fought several political campaigns on that theme, offering himself as mayor of a hypothetical free commune of Montmartre. From among the customers whom he insulted and despatched to the Institut, right at the back of the hall, and so called because the waiters wore the green palms of academicians on their suits, Salis distinguished his own friends and ushered

Shadow horsemen from a Napoleonic epic by Caran d'Ache

Poster for a café-restaurant, about 1890

Poster for l'Ane Rouge

(*left*) A poster by Steinlen for the Chat Noir

them into the best places. There were painters, like Toulouse-Lautrec and Anquetin and, later on, Bonnard and Vuillard, writers, the humorists Alphonse Allais and Maurice Donnay, and the poet Jean Moréas. When such purists as Robert de Montesquiou and Helleu ventured into the cabaret, they made mock of its motley decorations, and whenever they encountered the same vaguely Louis XIII furniture, church ornaments and candles in the studios of bad painters they dubbed it the 'style Chat Noir'. A Swiss Guard, halberd in hand, stood guard at the door.

Besides Salis, beating the big drum, was the publicist Emile Goudeau, a jovial native of Périgord, famous for his practical jokes, which included his own (fictitious) funeral conducted by the firm of Borniol in the Chat Noir transformed into a mortuary chapel. He had founded the club of the Hydrophates, because they drank massively in Montmartre, especially 'the green fairy', absinth. He would pay his associates in drink and the most gifted of them, Jules Jouy, died of it. Music was well represented at the Chat Noir by Charles de Sivery, Verlaine's brother-in-law, and by Delmet, 'emotional and springlike composer of adorable songs'. As for the plastic arts, they were given a new dimension with shadow plays with a commentary by Salis or by this or that poet, to a piano accompaniment. Henri Rivière's drawings, *La Marche des Rois* were already highly Symbolist, while the horsemen of Caran d'Ache, illustrating the Napoleonic legend, appealed to the public's patriotic feelings. The drawings of Willette, who was responsible for the large canvas at the back of the cabaret, were very eighteenth-century in inspiration, with sometimes rather macabre Pierrots. Pierrot is the poet, the disappointed lover, the everlasting dreamer, doomed to make the world laugh. Plenty of young and already disappointed poets saw themselves in him. It was a Pierrot who sang MacNab's celebrated ballad:

> Around the Chat Noir
> I seek my fortune . . .

The fame of the Chat Noir spread far beyond Montmartre. In Barcelona, in 1895, for instance, a Catalan bohemian, Pedro Romen, a friend of Salis and imitator of the *chansonnier* Bruant, opened an artistic cabaret called El Quatre Gats, complete with shadow play and songs. Pablo Ruiz Picasso used to meet his friends there. In Paris, the *chansonniers* invaded cafés, which, like the Chat Noir and the Grande Pinte before it, were in their turn making themselves look like studios, with lots of pictures on the wall. There was the Abbaye de Thélème in the Place Pigalle with its Renaissance décor, which was very expensive, and, very cheap, the Auberge du Clou where Eric Satie played the piano after quarrelling with Salis. Alfred Jarry was often there. Some of the Symbolists, deserting the left bank, were to be seen there. At the Ane Rouge, Georges de Feure, most elegant of the Symbolists, had painted some very Art Nouveau frescoes and Verlaine would hold forth before them. The Chat Noir and its imitators occasionally turned themselves into picture galleries to exhibit young artists who, like de Feure and Steinlen, became famous in 1900.

Degas: *L'Absinthe*, 1876. Paris, Louvre

(*overleaf*) Willette: Decoration for the Chat Noir

Alongside the cabarets that were multiplying on the Butte round about 1885, there were hordes of magazines, some of them comic and jokey, like the ones published by Rimbaud and Rollinat, but all with leanings towards the macabre: the *Hydrophate*, for instance, launched Emile Goudeau's poems on Satan. Others were metaphysical, open to the first essays in Symbolism, others again, like the *Décadent*, welcomed anarchists. There were also proto-Surrealists, like the *Incohérents*, who also had their own cabaret. Talent flourished in Montmartre and breathed life into a literature that was divided between Parnassian academicism and naturalism.

A number of reviews had a cabaret as their centre and emblem. Rodolphe Salis, of course, called his weekly the *Chat Noir*. Chansonniers, poets and artists all worked on it. In particular Caran d'Ache with his military scenes, for they were jingoistic on the Butte, and Willette with his Verlaine-like portrayals of weedy Pierrots and dubious Columbines with now and then a baby Jesus, because they were almost as Catholic as they were patriotic. This literary youth of Montmartre, which looked even more startling than the generation of 1830 had done, appalled the bourgeois and irritated the realists, the moderns, those who followed Zola and lived in the world. Art criticism was in the hands of Félix Fénéon, that austere young man with an impeccable style, a remarkable knowledge of modern painting and a sneaking sympathy with the anarchists.

The success of the *Chat Noir* magazine led to imitations: the *Courrier Français* lasted much longer than the *Chat Noir*, thanks to the talent for publicity of Jules Roques, director of a rival cabaret, the Abbaye de Thélème. This weekly began modestly at first in a back room of the Rat Mort which served as an editorial office. There, articles and drawings were discussed over innumerable glasses: 'Waiter, another green chartreuse for M. Lorrain!' And then there was the *Mirliton*, owned by the *chansonnier* Bruant.

For strolling about Montmartre, from cabarets to *bals publics*, Lorrain would wear a rakish suit of corduroy velvet with a red sash, the costume in which Bruant was immortalized by Lautrec. Those of his friends whose names have survived include the illustrator Henri Rivière; Le Cardonnel, later abbé, a nature poet; Maurice Rollinat, a more than Baudelairean poet – of the carrion kind; Léon Bloy; Emile Goudeau, briefly, and Marie Krynska, a poetess who claimed to be the inventor of free verse. And there were those whose names alone were notable in this nest of failures, like Alcanter de Brahame. As for these gentlemen's lady friends, Lorrain was to paint savage portraits of them when they adopted aesthetic attitudes without the means to sustain them, the Mimis of the Incohérents or Musettes of the Rat Mort.

The *bockeuse* woke one fine morning an inspired poetess, the muse of Cape Misery, pupil of Baudelaire and Jean Moréas, goddess of the saucer and Thalia of the small tip, and abruptly abandoning fat wallets for artistic writing and Byzantine epithets, she flew away – for the Muses have wings – to the heights of Rochechouart and that new Acropolis of the age, the Chat Noir.

Van Gogh: *Le Père Tanguy*, 1887. Paris, Musée Rodin

12

MOUNT LESBOS

— Sans les femmes, qu'est-ce qui nous resterait !...

Montmartre, the metropolis of anarchists, artists and all those who, irked by society's laws, elected to despise them, Montmartre, in the 1880s, became the great lesbian centre of Paris. No one there was surprised to see ladies in men's suits, with ties and trilbies, sitting at the café tables. In the Moulin Rouges and the Elysées it was quite acceptable for two women to waltz together, as Lautrec painted them, hatless, in men's jackets and open-necked shirts, clasping one another breast to breast – the best prelude to amorous enjoyment, as Proust's Professor Cottard explained, watching the young girls dancing at the Casino de Balbec. In this connection it may be noted that Montmartre has no place in the work of Proust. Zola, on the other hand, who once lived in the Boulevard de Clichy, knew Montmartre well, although he took no part in the pleasures to be got there. In *Nana*, he described a famous lesbian restaurant:

> They sat at a table in the very room where Laure Piédefer sat enthroned on the high bench of a cash desk. This Laure was a woman of fifty, her ample form squeezed into belts and corsets. Women came in, one after another, reached up across the saucers and kissed Laure on the lips with fond familiarity, while that monster, moist-eyed, endeavoured to divide her favours equally and so arouse no jealousy. The waitress, in contrast, was a tall, thin, ravaged-looking creature who served the ladies with lowered eyelids and a darkly flashing glance. The three rooms filled up quickly. There were about a hundred customers there, seated all at random round the tables. Most were nearing forty, huge women, thick and fleshy, with puffy cheeks sagging about slack lips, but amongst the bulging bosoms and stomachs there were a few slim, pretty girls to be seen, still with an air of innocence underneath their brazen manners, novices picked up in some dance hall and brought by a customer to Laure's, where the crowd of obese women, excited by the aroma of youth about them, courted them like fidgety old bachelors and jostled one another to buy them sweets.

Nana is set in the Second Empire but the naturalistic novelist went, notebook in hand, to La Souris in 1880 or so for his information. The proprietress of this establishment, who went by the name of Palmyre, was a friend of Toulouse-Lautrec, who would go there to observe the behaviour of the ladies. She had a bulldog and Lautrec made a drawing of it.

We may consult Jean Lorrain, who also visited Palmyre's: 'Some past their best, others still unripe, old, belated emigrées from Cythera to Lesbos, young women jealous of their beauty and made cautious through fear, they were all crowded round the *table d'hôtes* of the *quartier* Pigalle, along with stars from the operetta and ladies from the big top, all of them converted to the religion of practised, sterile embraces.' There were prostitutes, too, for whom Lesbos was only a sign like any other. They would meet there after 'doing' the corridors of the nearby music halls. Now and then some great lady come down in the world would turn up at the Souris, like the

Two lesbians at the Rat Mort: 'Without women what's left?' Drawing by Forain in the *Courrier Français*, 1898

Menu at the Rat Mort. Oscar Wilde was dismayed by its frugality

Colette and her friend the Marquise de Belbœuf in a show which caused a scandal

Marquise de Belboeuf, daughter of the Duc de Morny. Lorrain drew her, too:

From the bright, silken studios of women painters, where, among the fusukas, artists and models kiss one another lingeringly on the lips, to the great mirrored halls where flesh sells for anything from one louis to twenty-five, Elysée-Montmartre, Moulin Rouge and Folies-Bergère, she has seen it all, frequented it and plumbed it to the depths, erotomaniac tourist in Perversion, much more a slave to boredom, even, than to vice. Vicious – but does she even know it? And

Toulouse-Lautrec: *The two friends*, 1894. Albi, Musée Toulouse-Lautrec

Van Dongen: *The friends*. Los Angeles, Armand Hammer Foundation

yet she certainly has the mask, with her delicate profile with its sharp, arrogant bone structure, her pallid complexion, like a precocious schoolboy who has been reading too many of Virgil's idylls, her non-existent hips, flat bosom and all the equivocal yet charming aspect of the androgynous woman.

Fifteen years later, the marquise – Missy to her friends – met Colette in some more or less literary circle and took a fancy to the young woman who was just beginning her music-hall career in pantomime. After her divorce from Willy, the fat journalist who put his name to her first novels, Colette went to live near Mme de Belboeuf. The ladies lived in the sixteenth *arrondissement* and would go slumming in Montmartre to pick up 'chums'. 'Some cellars in Montmartre also sheltered these restless souls, haunted by their own loneliness, who would find some peace between the low walls, under the rough protection of a temporary partner, to the oily sizzling of a real *fondue vaudoise* and with a bellowing contralto to sing them the love songs of Augusta Holmes.' That passage is taken from one of Colette's later books, *Ces Plaisirs*, subtitled 'which are lightly called physical'.

Drugs, love affairs with men or women, the novelist listened to confidences and made them moving, without taking away their sordid side: the smell of cheap soap in *hôtels de passe*, unmade beds and make-up smudged with tears. Colette knew all these in a *quartier* which was, as they said at the time, consecrated to vice, for in the first years of this century Montmartre had lost much of its charm for artists; new blocks threw their shadows over the narrow streets and already it was a *quartier* that lived by night, like a much-painted beauty only able to preserve the illusion by artificial light. The marquise, who was something of a blue-stocking, wrote scripts for pantomimes for Colette. She even wanted to appear on stage with her. And in January 1907 there were to be seen posters emblazoned with the arms of Morny, announcing *Le Rêve d'Egypte* at the Moulin Rouge, 'by Madame the Marquise de Morny with Colette and Yssim'. Yssim, of course, was Missy. It caused a huge scandal, since a part of society was descended from Napoleon's marshals and connected with the Bonapartes. The marquise was obliged to find someone to replace her and Colette, after a poor reception, went off to play the *Rêve d'Egypte* in the provinces. Out of this experience, like a good housewife letting nothing go to waste, she wrote a fine book, *L'Envers du Music Hall*. The marquise, ruined and alone, lived off the charity of Sacha Guitry. She committed suicide in 1944.

By 1885, there were other places besides the Souris where lesbians used to meet: the Hanneton in the Rue Pigalle and the Rat Mort in the Place Pigalle. It was possible to lunch there, extremely badly, for two francs. 'They have to justify the price,' wrote Oscar Wilde, who did not repeat the experience. One curious character, a prolific poet and shocking novelist, Catulle Mendès, was very much at home in these cabarets, where he found material for his narratives. Baudelaire had said of him: 'I like that lad, he has all the vices.' And for forty years, Mendès devoted himself to

(*right*) Toulouse-Lautrec: *Divan Japonais*, 1893. Poster

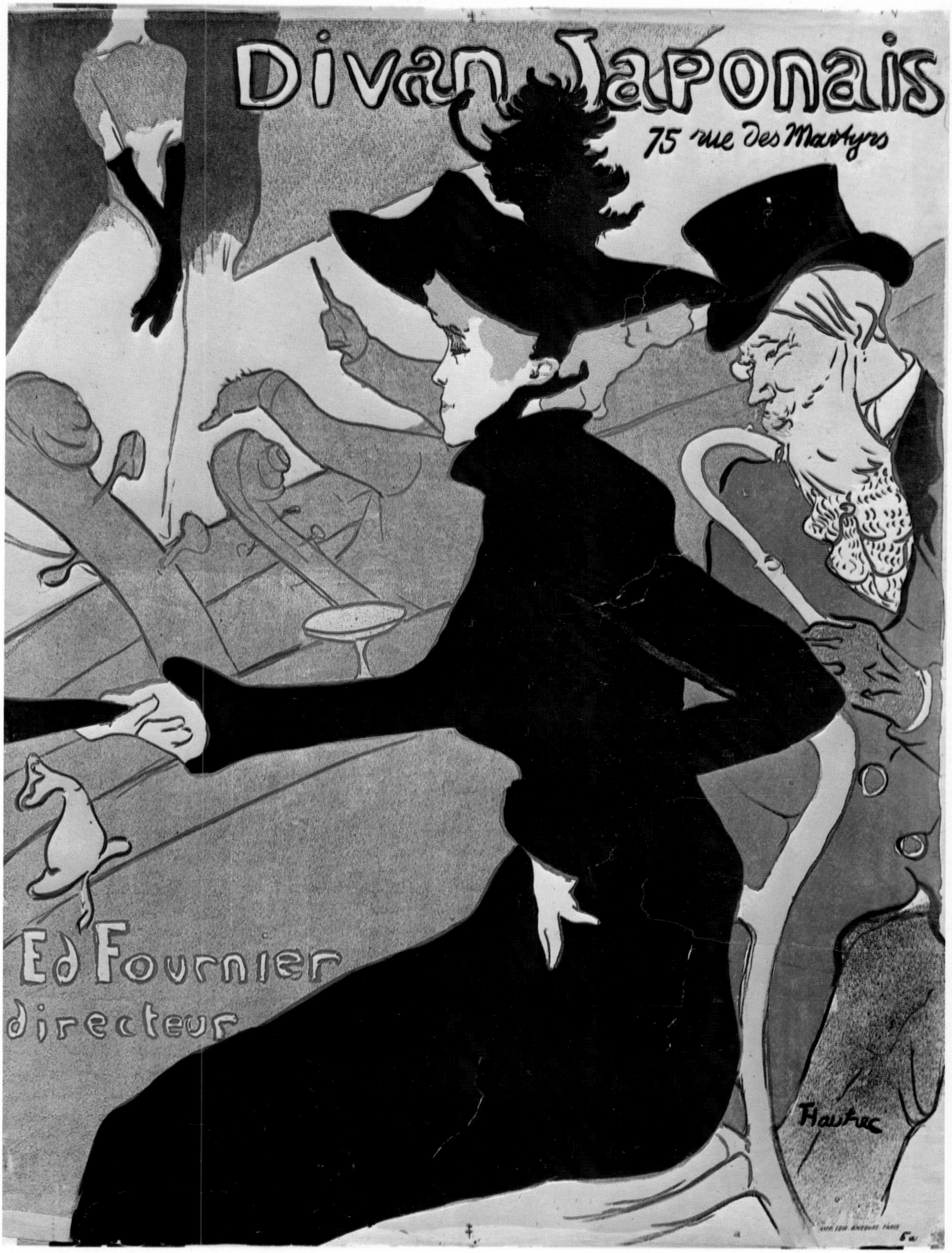
Divan Japonais
75 rue des Martyrs
Ed Fournier
directeur

ensuring that the poet spoke the truth. By 1880 he was living with the Augusta Holmes mentioned by Colette. She was a splendid, half-Irish blonde who wrote music which was very popular at the time. Her *Hymn to Love* might have been the *Marseillaise* of Lesbos:

> *Vers elles, vers elles,*
> *Amour, conduis-nous en battant des ailes.*
> *Vers elles, vers elles,*
> *Les blondes, les blanches, les belles,*
> *Vers elles, plus loin, là-bas, plus loin encore,*
> *Vers elles, vers elles, les vierges aux cheveux d'or.*

> To them, to them,
> Love, lead us with beating wings.
> To them, to them,
> The blonde, the white, the fair,
> To them, far off, away there, and yet further still,
> To them, to them, the virgins with their golden hair.

Renoir painted a very fine picture of her daughters at the piano, but Augusta Holmes's great friend was a woman painter, Louise Abbema, who, when young, looked like a rajah and in her old age like a Japanese admiral, possibly owing to the influence of her studio which was decorated in the Japanese style, with painted screens, fans on the walls, black lacquered furniture and here and there a Buddha. The little actresses flocked to this studio, driven by two ambitions: to be painted by Louise Abbema and to meet Sarah Bernhardt, who permitted the lady to worship her.

The lesbians were so well established a feature of Montmartre that, painting the *Bal du Moulin Rouge* in 1901, Picasso put in two women embracing in the foreground.

Seurat: *Study for Chahut*, 1889–90. London, Courtauld Institute Galleries

13
THE MOULIN ROUGE

Just as the name of Renoir still attaches to the Moulin de la Galette, so that of Toulouse-Lautrec is bound up with the Moulin Rouge. No more than fifteen years lie between Renoir's masterpiece and Lautrec's, the *quartier* is the same and yet what a difference! Between the customers of the Moulin de la Galette and those of the Moulin Rouge there is all the difference between simple pleasure and vice. By 1890 the exploitation of vice was beginning to assume a very businesslike appearance; not only were there brothels at home to be provided for, but establishments abroad had to be supplied as well, and Parisiennes were very much in demand. This was the period of the white slave trade and, underneath its frivolous surface, the Moulin Rouge was both a market and an exchange. The Milieu, with its collusion between police and criminals and its systematic exploitation of sexual pleasures, had become an organized business.

The Bal du Moulin Rouge opened on 5 October 1889 at 90 Boulevard de Clichy. There had never been a windmill there at all, only a cheap dance hall, the Reine Blanche. Charles Zidler, who was responsible for the show, did the thing in grand style, in order to outdo the Elysée-Montmartre. The dance hall was as big as a railway station and the din like a circus band; but although there was dancing people went there chiefly to see the chahut danced by the professionals whose choreography was the delight of connoisseurs. Out in the garden, there was drinking at little tables round an enormous cardboard elephant which could hold an entire orchestra, and there were monkeys on chains to amuse the customers. There was more drinking in the galleries surrounding the dance floor, where the dancers waited for their partners and their clients. The stage attractions included singers, both realistic and sentimental, and exotic dances, but the greatest draw of all was the *pétomane*. The vulgar nicknames of the cancan dancers, Grille d'Egoût, La Môme Fromage, Nini Patte en l'air, made the customers feel that they were really in the underworld. Their partner, Valentin, known as Le Désossé (Boneless) on account of his contortions, did not belong to the Milieu, but was the owner of a small café in the neighbourhood. And the music! Or rather the din, at a time when no means of sound amplification yet existed! The job of deafening the public with the famous tunes of Offenbach and Olivier Metra was entrusted to slide trombones, bass drums and cymbals. Then, by 1900, came the mattchiche and the cakewalk. On some nights the Moulin Rouge attained a bacchic frenzy that amazed foreign visitors. A reporter from the English magazine the *Pick Me Up*, who was certainly not strait-laced, could still write:

When the hours grow late the scene becomes almost indescribable. The slumbering passions of dancers are roused by their frequent visits to the refreshment tables, and in this place no passions need be curbed. There is shouting and horse-play; women are carried round the Hall on the shoulders of men; there is one fierce increasing cry for drink. A man dressed as a toreador, and whose face reminds me of that worn by Luis Mazzantini – no doubt Spain's

Place Blanche: the Moulin Rouge

One of Toulouse-Lautrec's panels for the Elysée-Montmartre reproduced in the *Mirliton*

The French cancan, about 1910

Cancan at the Moulin Rouge. Drawing by Manuel in the Pick Me Up, 1895

Dance hall of the Moulin Rouge. Photograph taken in about 1910

great matador will be flattered – passes me with a woman sitting on his shoulders. Her arms are round his neck, her coarse face is unredeemed by one solitary sign of even dormant intelligence. The Hall is clearing for a final quadrille, perhaps – as danced by the professional dancers – the strangest and most characteristic dance to be seen in this strange den. The solemn, ponderous way in which these women are indecent, the anxious crowd that surrounds each set six deep to make certain of seeing anything especially risky, the excitement of everybody save the performers – all these things combine to make a quadrille memorable.

Curiously, in less than thirty years, the cancan had become a kind of ritual dance, a vaguely erotic ceremonial in which it was less important for the priestesses to be young and pretty than skilled in performing the rite which ended in the splits.

From then on, an illuminated red windmill hung above the boulevard, like the lamp of a vast brothel. In fact, it was the biggest market for prostitution in Europe; for all their vulgar clothes, the girls there were almost as expensive as those in the Champs-Elysées. Frilled and feathered *cocottes* were not above coming to compete with them. The clientele was made up of gay dogs, gentlemen whose whole business was pleasure-seeking, sons of good families enjoying a little slumming and nervous, excited provincials. There were many foreigners, Russians and English especially, but also Rumanians, Levantines and South Americans, who added an exotic touch to this shady setting. Some society figures went there too, but the poster was exaggerating when it promised that this was '*le rendez-vous du High Life*'.

From the start, Toulouse-Lautrec went to the Moulin Rouge several times a week with his friends, upper-class men like himself, with an interest in painting, men like Joyant and Guibert. There he would meet the painter Anquetin and the caricaturist, Métivet. Lautrec's pictures were very often on exhibition in the foyer. Cheret had done the poster for the opening, but it was Lautrec whom Zidler asked for the poster for the 1891 season, which saw the début of a young dancer pinched from the Elysée-Montmartre, a handsome twenty-year-old called La Goulue. That poster put the name of the artist and of the dancer before all Paris.

'Now then, never seen a woman before?' Thrusting through the crowd of loafers, swaggerers and gaping provincials lining her route, La Goulue, plump, white and moulded into her little black stuff dress, sweeps coolly through the herd and, one hand resting on the shoulder of La Môme Fromage, lets her gaze roam insolently over all those rutting males with all the assurance of a beautiful woman who has seen it all before. The scene is the garden of the Elysée, the mirrored Moulin Rouge. . . . La Goulue! Springing out of a tumbled froth of skirts, of swirling lace and expensive undergarments trimmed with delicately coloured ribbons, a leg appears, pointing straight up to the chandelier: a leg held stiff and straight, gleaming silkily, clipped above the knee by a garter of diamonds; and the leg quivers, witty and gay, voluptuous and full of promise, with its mobile, disjointed foot seeming to wave to the packed throng of onlookers all round. The *Chahut* and the *Chahutoirs*, those vast meeting places of idlers and whores, La Goulue is the star of them: the star of Montmartre risen in the moonlight of Willette's Pierrot over the Sacré-Cœur, and the ghostly sails of long-gone windmills, a tinsel glory, both freakish and sordid, a gutter bloom caught in the beam of an electric light and suddenly taken up by fashion.

(Jean Lorrain)

La Goulue's success was immense but short-lived. Five years later she was exhibiting herself in a fairground booth for which her friend Lautrec had painted two large panels. She took to drink, or rather she drank more than ever, and finished up in 1929 as a tramp, after working as a servant in a brothel and selling sweets outside the

La Goulue, Grille d'Egout, Valentin Le Désossé and a friend doing the cancan at the Moulin Rouge, about 1880

Jane Avril. Poster by Toulouse-Lautrec, 1893

(*right*) Toulouse-Lautrec: *Jane Avril dancing*, about 1892. Paris, Louvre

Photograph of Toulouse-Lautrec wearing ceremonial Japanese costume

Photograph of Toulouse-Lautrec

Moulin Rouge. The life of a cancan dancer required a good deal of alcohol one way and another, what with the need for energy and encouraging the customers to drink.

By the time the Moulin Rouge opened, Lautrec was already a character in Montmartre. He had settled there in the summer of 1884, with his friends the Greniers at 19 Rue Fontaine, where he was close to the studios he frequented in turn, those of Léon Bonnat and Fernand Cormon, the latter a charming person who specialized in prehistoric scenes. In 1886, the Comte de Toulouse-Lautrec bought his son a studio in a brand-new building at 27 Rue Caulaincourt, which instantly became an amazing jumble with the parody of Puvis de Chavannes's *Bois Sacré* looming over all. There were Japanese fabrics and objects, paper sunshades, and the bearded midget was fond of dressing up as a Samurai or even as a geisha. An enormous easel half-filled the room and on it, for a long time, could be seen the *Ecuyère du Cirque Fernando* which afterwards hung in the hall of the Moulin Rouge.

Toulouse-Lautrec: *La Goulue and Valentin waltzing*. Lithograph, 1894

(*left*) Toulouse-Lautrec: *La Goulue at the Moulin Rouge*. Poster, 1891

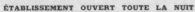

Publicity brochure by Chéret for a restaurant in the Place Blanche, 1895

The painter's family included enough eccentrics for there to be no objection to his vocation, only a cousin who came to visit his studio did once sigh: 'If only you wouldn't paint women of Montmartre!' There was a bar in one corner, with bottles of every description; having learned to make cocktails from an American friend, Lautrec never tired of inventing fearsome ones. Not that this prevented him sitting at café tables imbibing absinth, the 'green fairy' beloved of Verlaine, which was the favourite poison of Montmartre. In 1891, while still keeping on the studio, Lautrec went to live with a good friend, Dr Bourges, at 19 bis Rue Fontaine. His escapades more often ended up on the divan in the studio than in bed at the apartment.

Toulouse-Lautrec: *Quadrille at the Moulin Rouge*, 1892. Washington, National Gallery of Art

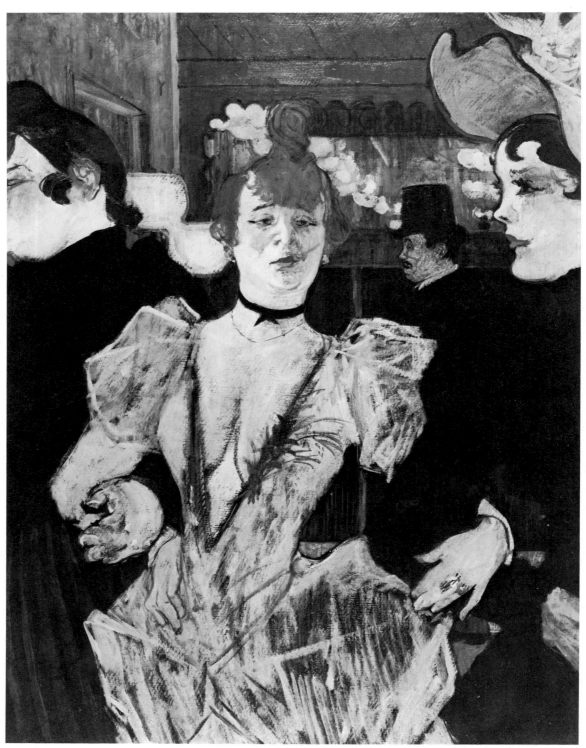

Toulouse-Lautrec: *La Goulue at the Moulin Rouge*, 1891–2. New York, Museum of Modern Art

(*right*) Toulouse-Lautrec: *Dance at the Moulin Rouge*, 1894. Philadelphia, Henry P. McIlhenny

In spite of his looks, Lautrec had some very pretty girls, he was so gay and could be kind, when he was not being malicious. He could also adopt a lordly tone which impressed these simple souls. There are still photographs of these women in existence and they are much more attractive than in Lautrec's canvases; very often they were the passing fancies of a friend and one, Maria, when she took to painting, became known under the name of Suzanne Valadon: we have met her already in the studios of Renoir and Degas. She tried to win Toulouse-Lautrec's affections and even to make him marry her by feigning suicide. The trick did not work and he dropped her. Yet he liked her, with her air of wickedness. Valadon, for her part, got on very well with the midget, for nature had endowed him so generously that he was nicknamed 'the coffeepot'. The talk at the Moulin Rouge was coarse and Lautrec's wit was both cruel and obscene. One day he saw a girl known for her willingness to oblige with oral sex come in with a swollen face. 'Pregnant?' the painter inquired simply.

He had other girls, other models who were called Carmen la Rousse and Lily la Rosse. When it was fine, Lautrec would make them pose in a garden belonging to a M. Forest at the back of the Boulevard de Clichy. Part of this garden was destroyed to make the bridge spanning the Montmartre cemetery and the rest in about 1930 to build the enormous Gaumont cinema, since demolished in its turn to make way for a hotel. Most famous of all Lautrec's models was Casque d'Or, a girl out of the gutter whose man was an anarchist and occasional murderer called Liaubeuf, who ended on the scaffold. In Becker's fine film, sympathetically telling Casque d'Or's story, Simone Signoret had exactly the type of vulgar beauty that attracted Lautrec, a *beauté de pétroleuse*, as the bourgeois, excited by the 'panthers of the faubourgs', put it.

We find the faces of all Lautrec's friends in the backgrounds of his pictures. Slipping in among the women and the dancers are the police, conspicuously disguised in bowler hats and drooping moustaches, and it is easy to guess at the collusion, the blackmail and the occasional blind eye that passed between these policemen and the Milieu. In the oils and pastels we can see the madams offering young and more or less unspoiled girls to old, thickly painted gentlemen dressed in grand but slightly soiled clothes and ready for any kind of liaison. To others they are pointing out those whose speciality is whipping, the English vice, who can be recognized by their stern looks. Then there are the lesbians, knowing quite well that the girls often like to forget in their arms the men who keep them. The young pimps are usually brilliant dancers, launching their sisters into the world while overseeing the two or three women who work for them; and, more sinister, the tanned, scarred face and probably tattooed body of the pimp come back from Biribi, the military prison, and ready to become the 'terror' of a *quartier*. Then again, there are the imitators of Valentin le Désossé. Lorrain has sketched the kind of little drama which can be divined in more than one of Lautrec's canvases:

Toulouse-Lautrec: *The Englishman at the Moulin Rouge*, 1892. Lithograph

Toulouse-Lautrec: *La Goulue dancing with Valentin le Désossé*, 1895. Paris, Louvre

This dancer, surely her lover, had left her and, a little way off, swaggering carelessly in a worn velvet suit, with chest out and pointed toe, was capering about the dance floor like a loose colt, seizing the women round the waist and twirling them round like so many tops, one after another, they thrilled and excited, he standing well back on his heels. And the one he had deserted, the woman with her hair parted in two black wings, her face set and her eyes hard, watched and observed him, studied him with a dull misery and rising anger; the other women had formed a circle and now he was footing it alone, over-excited,

throwing up his legs and kicking up his feet. He hitched up his coat-tails, swung his hips, bowed to the ground before the pale, silent girl and, bottom up, like someone playing leapfrog, let his laughing face peep teasingly between his legs, then went on to perform still more contortions. (*Monsieur de Phocas*)

The same cast, intermingled with a more bourgeois public, was to be found in the promenades of the music halls. There, Toulouse-Lautrec rubbed shoulders with his models and made a quick sketch of this or that comic or charming figure as it appeared in the rosy light of the gangway. The biggest music hall was the Casino de Paris in the Rue de Clichy, half-way between Montmartre and the fashionable quarters. It was opened in 1892 and became a serious rival to the Moulin Rouge. The painter preferred the more intimate Divan Japonais at 17 Rue des Martyrs, for which he designed his famous poster (*see opposite p. 94*), being somewhat in love with the star, Jane Avril, a tall, fair girl who danced in the costume of an English chorus girl and sometimes sang a verse or two. She was an amazing creature, with more charm than talent. Her friend, May Belfort (another poster), had little enough of either. If these women were a success, they would be engaged by the Moulin Rouge or one of the establishments in the Champs-Elysées; if not, they went into the popular music halls that were springing up all along the Boulevard Rochechouart towards the Porte de la Chapelle. In these Alcazars, Eldorados and Bouffes du Nord, they were the *poseuses*, who had frequently inspired Degas to more than one pastel, and Lorrain to a passage like this:

On stage there are plump, full-fleshed women, grouped in a circle and displaying their bosoms in the legendary, old-fashioned 'basket of fruit' which has vanished from the café-concerts today. Their breasts powdered with flour, the lower halves of their faces slashed, like a red gash, by the moist paint on their lips; this is the shop-window, the dull, sexual shop-window. Each in her turn, the puppets rise and bleat out a song, or quiver with sudden animation in time to the music of the zoo.

The audience was on the same level as the show:

And all the dregs of an audience made up of bourgeois citizens and petty clerks applauded, tickled by the dubious transvestite show. The grotesqueness of men got up as women excited them quite as much as the plump buttocks of pretty girls crammed into soldiers' tunics. And over all this display of flesh decked out in tawdry costumes, all the underarm hair of the blondes and the warmly shaded necks of boyish brunettes, the pathetic troupe of artistes went on and off, shedding more and more clothes with every scene, growing more and more naked with every act, a walking display of bodies fat and thin, bedizened with sweat and paint.

May Belfort by Toulouse-Lautrec. Cleveland, Museum of Art

14
THE SONGS

All the representatives of the assorted life of Montmartre became, from 1880, to some extent legendary characters, thanks to two *chansonniers*, who were assured more than a merely fashionable success by the posters of Toulouse-Lautrec. They were Aristide Bruant and Yvette Guilbert. These two stars made the *chanson* an acknowledged art and reaped enormous rewards. All this came from the success of the Chat Noir; there had certainly been popular singers before, like that Thérésa who was famous during the Second Empire, but for the first time real poets were writing the songs. Bruant was a Burgundian peasant who came to Paris and got into bad company. Hear him describing his beginnings:

> Spontaneously, he began spouting argot, his teachers being the strollers he met in the streets in the course of long forays about the outer boulevards. He wrote a few monologues in argot and recited them with some success at small amateur concerts. He established his cabaret in the old home of the Chat Noir among a profusion of assorted junk and hung sketches by Steinlen and pictures by Toulouse-Lautrec on the walls. From ten o'clock at night to two in the morning he would recite affecting verses or bawl out vengeful choruses, making the whole audience join in the refrains. In between times, he would welcome the army, drink with the academy, abuse boors, denounce fools and apostrophize the authorities of the day.

Bruant was a well-built fellow who borrowed the workers' black corduroy jacket, red sash and boots and the artists' broad-brimmed hat and long red scarf. He very soon made his mark, with the aid of a good deal of impudence. In his raucous voice, Bruant would insult the bourgeois who applauded him and saw him as the Villon of the *fin de siècle*. After all, he sang about prostitutes and rogues and his ballads often enough ended on the scaffold. Yet he could be sentimental when singing of Montmartre:

> One autumn night it seems,
> While the old butte was taking off
> Her dress of green
> We were wedded in the hay,
> No mayor, no wedding feast, no witnesses,
> In Montmartre.

Bruant's cabaret, called the Mirliton, was never anything but crowded. When he went down to sing at the Ambassadeurs in the Champs-Elysées, he insisted on using Toulouse-Lautrec's poster, which made the artist's name outside Montmartre. But the artist who is inseparable from Bruant is the cartoonist who illustrated his songs, Théophile-Alexandre Steinlen.

Steinlen, a native of the Vaud canton, came to Montmartre in 1881, when he was twenty-two, in company with a seamstress whom he finally married, and stayed there for the rest of his life. *L'Assommoir* made a deep impression on him and he would

Toulouse-Lautrec: *Yvette Guilbert: Linger Longer Loo!'* Lithograph, 1898

Poster for the realist singer Eugénie Buffet by Métivet

Toulouse-Lautrec's poster for Aristide Bruant in the Champs-Elysées, 1893

Rochegrosse's poster for *Louise*, illustrating the famous duo overlooking the lights of Paris

draw the working girls and their lovers with a bold, lithographic line. Anatole France, who commissioned him to illustrate his novel *Crainquebille* (the story of a Montmartre tramp), saw in Steinlen's drawings, 'the bright, morning stream, the dark night stream of working men and women, the groups seated at tables on the pavement, which the wine seller of the time called the terrace, the men and women who prowled the boulevards by night, grave or gay, the soul of the crowd had entered into him'. As a painter of the workaday world, Steinlen is close to Eugène Carrière and to the sculptor Constantin Meunier. He was a close friend of the anarchist Jean Grave and his most savage drawings appeared in the *Chat Noir* and afterwards in the *Assiette au Beurre*. In gentler mood, he illustrated some charming songs by Paul Delmet, singer of the loves of working girls and artists on the Butte.

After the realistic and cynical Bruant, came the realistic and despairing Jehan Rictus, who

> arose like a Christ of the faubourgs, a tall, melancholy being with a pale, emaciated face, thin and narrow-shouldered, elongated, like a tear drop, and with such a weariness in his eyes! Every night at the Quatzarts, Jehan Rictus speaks what is perhaps the finest argot poem of grief of our time. The *chanson*, from mocking, became by turns plaintive and savage. Bruant had already dwelt with horror on the sinister Paris of pimps and prostitutes, now it was the wretchedness of the poor, the hunger, thirst and cold that they eternally endured, that the Muse of Montmartre had gathered up in her apron, like a housewife scooping up an urchin lost at a street corner. (Jean Lorrain)

There are still singers in Montmartre who declaim Rictus's most lugubrious verses in front of audiences gorged with the most expensive food who dare not protest.

With Yvette Guilbert there was little sentiment, only sneers and occasional hysterical laughter. She knew how to choose her lyric writers, Maurice Donnay, Alphonse Allais, Xanrof and Lorrain. Lorrain's articles did as much to launch Yvette Guilbert as Toulouse-Lautrec's poster; both had applauded her début at the Divan Japonais, a tiny music hall in the Rue des Martyrs. And how close Lorrain comes to Lautrec in this description:

> Long, long, long, long and thin, her breast chalk-white and curved like a young boy's, but with so little bosom that her dress can plunge as far as it may; fragile arms, very long and trailing, gloved in long black kid, like supple scarves; a body that seems ready to slip off her shoulders; the slenderest of necks; and, poised upon that body, at once graceful and languid, like a great woman of the world, a small head with irregular features, short nose and eyes like great gaping holes, outrageously mascara'd, but the brow an exquisite oval haloed in an adorable head of ash-blond hair. Her diction is precise and crisp; words and phrases issue from her carmine-painted lips, uttered with a marvellous clarity as though cut

out with scissors. No special voices – but funny intonations, subtle nuances, very cleverly done. The most original thing about this sophisticated music hall singer is her correctness, the almost rigid stillness of that lanky, overgrown schoolgirl's body, her absence of gesture contrasting with the frantic rolling of her eyes and all the aggravated miming of that pallid, tormented clown's face.

Like Bruant, Yvette Guilbert had known poverty and would tell those who paid highly to hear her harsh truths in a voice that alternated between the peasant's harshness and the shrill tones of the faubourg. In 1896 she made a triumphal tour of the United States, putting even Sarah Bernhardt temporarily in the shade and adding to the dubious fame of Montmartre. In Vienna, she aroused the admiration of

(*above and left*) Drawings by Steinlen in the *Mirliton*

Jacques Villon: Poster for the Guinguette Fleurie, a rendezvous for singers

Cover by de Feure for a collection by the singer Xavier Privas: *Chimères et Grimaces*

Gustave Charpentier's study reconstructed in the Musée du Vieux-Montmartre

Professor Freud, who remained a loyal friend. Yvette Guilbert had been discovered by Zidler who wanted to make a circus rider of the slim, lovely girl. But Yvette very soon preferred singing and he started her off at the Moulin Rouge.

So many songs led at last to an opera, *Louise* by Gustave Charpentier. In it we find all the old legends of Montmartre. The working girl in love with a young painter, the prostitutes and the anarchist father. All this to a full orchestra playing a score that is a jumble of everything from Wagner to Massenet. *Louise* was written between 1890 and 1894 by a young composer who had settled in Montmartre on his return from Rome. The low-life side of the work caused the Opéra to hesitate for a long time: if only the composer would have agreed to have *Louise* put on in romantic costume! But Charpentier, faithful to his naturalistic principles, refused even to cut out the argot words from his libretto, foreshadowing in this the early work of Brecht. The opera was performed at last on 2 February 1900. The audience was less troubled by the fact that the singer Mary Garden had a slight English accent than by the socialist tendency of the work as a whole. The theme of the song *V'la le plaisir, Mesdames*, repeated as a leitmotiv pleased the Wagnerians, while the aesthetes applauded Jussaume's sets, including a panoramic view of Paris in the dusk. *Louise* was put on by opera houses all over the world, setting the seal of artistic respectability on Montmartre. For many people, the by now thoroughly old-fashioned charm of *Louise* remains inseparable from the fame of Montmartre. Thus Carl Van Vechten recalled gazing out of the window of the restaurant Le Savoyard,

> the broad windows of which look out over pretty much all the north-east quarter of Paris, now a glittering labyrinth of lights set in an obscure sea of darkness. It was not far from here that Louise and Julien were living together when they were interrupted by Louise's mother; and it was looking down towards these lights that they swore those eternal vows ending with Louise's 'c'est une féerie' and Julien's correction, 'non, c'est la vie'.   (*Sacred and Profane Memories*)

Montmartre is still the capital of the *chanson*. There are *chansonniers* of a very intimate kind, with piano and shaded lamps, broad *chansonniers* in imitation country inns and political *chansonniers* in little theatres where they delight provincials with their references to the latest scandals. Their political line tends to be to the right, while still retaining a mildly anarchistic side to it. But in all these places the *chansonniers* are obliged to keep singing the successful songs of Bruant and Yvette Guilbert and the sentimental melodies of Delmet, to please audiences who still believe in the myth of Montmartre.

15
MOUNT BYZANTIUM

MORPHINE
par Matignon
Cl. Fiorillo

Nowhere can the two streams supplying the intellectual *fin de siècle* be seen more clearly than in Montmartre. The materialist stream which attracted the weary aesthetes who, from Degas to Toulouse-Lautrec, bestowed a down-to-earth, occasionally sordid beauty on the Moulin Rouge, and the idealistic stream which turned its back on the everyday and exploited the imagination, preferring Puvis de Chavannes to Toulouse-Lautrec. Lautrec painted a parody of *Le Bois Sacré*, inserting art students among the muses, and demonstrating the incongruity of such a connection. But such contrasts were no surprise to anyone on the Butte, for a large section of its population had discovered that idealism was a salable commodity. The background to this shoddy mysticism was Byzantine, like the Sacré-Cœur. The Chat Noir had set the example. Its dance hall was decorated, 'with a wrought-iron chandelier of the Byzantine school, presented to Rodolphe Salis by the Emperor of Brazil in return for a set of the *Chat Noir* bound according to the method of the monks of Puteaux' (*The Chat Noir Guide*). Byzantine in intention, if not in style, with its complicated allegories castigating the wickedness inseparable from bourgeois wealth, was Willette's great stained glass window called *Te Deum Laudamus*, full of suggestive artistry and wonderful colouring. In the centre is Fortune, a golden calf leaning up against the guillotine, Poverty dragging on the legs of Poetry (a cripple can still sing), while Beauty proffers her lover Pierrot's head upon a charger and Death beats time frenziedly. By 1895, the mystical cabarets were overtaking the realist ones. Abel Hermant, who was one of the best social commentators of the period, takes us, in one of his novels, into such a cabaret trading in the ideal. The resident poet, author of a notorious piece of pleading on behalf of incest, but since converted, declaims a mystico-libertarian work depicting the guilt and remorse of one who, starving, had stolen some communion wafers. This long, familiar address to Christ is the forerunner of all hippie writing. Anarchy went hand in hand with neo-catholicism at the foot of the Sacré-Cœur, which was rising slowly enough to picture the gigantic dome glittering with mosaics. One showman, Jules Roque, understood this very well when he founded a rival journal to the *Chat Noir*, the *Courrier Français*, with illustrations by Steinlen, Rops and Willette. Lorrain's savage articles ran side by side with the preposterous stories of Alphonse Allais. There were the ravings of Léon Bloy, a Catholic driven to distraction by any remotely liberal measure introduced by the Church, like the anchorites who heaped abuse on Theodora. One has only to read the advertisements in the *Courrier Français* to see how esoteric cliques were multiplying around 1890. For instance, the Rosicrucians organized a number of conferences in Montmartre. Numerous clairvoyantes moved in, some, aspiring only to tell the fortunes of prostitutes and concierges, dealt their greasy cards in basements smelling of cats; others, got up in flowing robes, and with oriental names, gazed into their crystal balls in a room reeking of incense for the benefit of smart folk come in quest of an ideal – or else by way of an inquest on past goings-on. There are still a great many fortune tellers in Montmartre.

Matignon: *Morphine*. A great success at the 1907 Salon. It shows three *demi-mondaines* trying the fashionable drug for which Montmartre had become the chief market

In 1893 Huysmans's terrible novel *Là-Bas* set the fashion for black masses, and Jules Roque, with Lorrain's assistance, organized a grand monastic banquet, very lewd and pagan. For our Montmartre Byzantines loved dressing up. But there was no longer anything in the spirit of the Moulin de la Galette or the Moulin Rouge, such frolics were left to the common herd and the artists had to take part in pseudo-historical rites. And by then what was meant by 'artist' was anyone who dabbled with

Medieval ball organized by the *Courrier Français* at the Elysée-Montmartre in 1893

a palette or a keyboard, anyone who wrote verse or recited it. There were the models, the students from the Conservatoire, hopeless failures still with their little circle of admirers, all dressed up according to their most secret dreams to enjoy a luxurious bacchanal. The Bal des Quatzarts, planned in the studios of the Ecole des Beaux-Arts, was held at the Moulin Rouge, cleared of its usual attractions for the night and decorated by the students. Let us follow Lorrain into the most sumptuous of these masquerades:

Café des Décadents, Rue Fontaine. Drawing by Heidbrinck in the *Courrier Français* in 1890

Everyone was crowded in front of the boxes or parading up and down draped in exotic rags and costume jewellery, in assorted groups of alluring models and young art students: Hamlet and Romeo, Knights of Malta or of the Round Table, all the Tristans and Tannhausers, all the Elsas and all the princesses of Germany, Italy and Scotland, and in the middle of the crowd was the parade of splendid nudes presented in the ingenious tableaux dreamed up by every studio. And then there was the black mass with its naked woman, staring ecstatically, stretched out on a cross of black velvet amid the flickering light of candles, and at her feet the frantic, kneeling figure of a bishop, swinging a sacrilegious censer over the idol. And after the penitents and the inquisitors of this accursed procession, came the triumphant Peacock Woman and her brilliant portrayal of Venus crouching in the shimmering circle, emerald and lapis lazuli, of an immense peacock's tail.

Cabaret de l'Enfer, Boulevard de Clichy, Montmartre, 1900 (*detail opposite*)

Up until 1950 Montmartre retained an aura of evil for provincials and foreign visitors, and did its best to satisfy them with a tawdry kind of satanism. The most famous of these places, in the Boulevard de Clichy, was called L'Enfer. The entrance was decorated with plaster of Paris women plunging into cardboard flames and you went in through a huge, gaping devil mouth. Inside, waiters dressed as skeletons made the most of the darkness to serve undrinkable drinks. On the stage, the singer belting out lugubrious couplets alternated with scenes of torment. Rather middle-aged girls, half-undressed, pretended to be whipped and hurled into boiling oil by yelling devils, all with an air of total boredom that was really the next thing to hell. Next door was the cabaret of heaven, with a Gothic façade, where the drinks were served by barefoot angels in nightdresses with make-believe wings. There was also a cabaret *du Néant* (of Limbo). The decline of religious faith, which deprived the blasphemy of its spice, and the speculators who wanted the sites of the cabarets to

Georges de Feure drew these fantastic costumes for a ball organized by the *Courrier Français*

Quelques Costumes pour le Bal du « Courrier Français ».   Par de Feure.

build a block of flats brought about the end of these last witnesses to Montmartre's esoteric phase.

If a mixture of piety and viciousness, cultural refinement and superstition, may be called Byzantine, then the most Byzantine character in Montmartre from 1904 onwards was Max Jacob, a Jew born in Brittany – a contradiction of a kind that was to run all through his life. As a young man, he was looked up to as a master by writers very little his juniors. The novelist Roland Dorgelès, for example, never forgot his first visit to Max.

> The smell of ether and incense pervaded everything, as though in the chapels of black masses. I did not know where to sit down, there were clothes on the bed and on the chairs, the table was cluttered with bottles, tubes, cups and household utensils. Shoes had a bag of roast chestnuts in them and a gouache was drying in front of the stove. The confusion had even spread to the walls where the signs of the zodiac were all muddled up with weird maxims and friends' addresses. Before long there would be the addition of a circle drawn in blue chalk to mark the place where the holy Face of Christ had appeared to him in a vision which brought about his conversion. The toilet arrangements were concealed behind a screen no junk dealer would have given forty sous for. It was painted by Picasso.

To earn a living, Max Jacob told fortunes for the local concierges and he also painted gouaches copied from picture postcards and sold them to the tourists. In the evenings he would amuse a gathering of friends in a studio by doing imitations of a bad music hall: the barefoot dancer, the singer of patriotic songs. On his way home he would pick up the most undesirable characters and find in the disgust which seized him in the morning the strength to go rushing to Saint-Jean l'Evangéliste to confess. This church would have seemed more like a trades union building but for its late Symbolist decorations. It was considered daring. That was at the time when Max Jacob saw Christ appear to him in his attic room in September 1909.

16
THE ENGLISH

Paris during the Second Empire was the city of easy pleasures for the wealthy English – and there were many who settled there. Along with the Russians, they made the fortunes of the great restaurants and the famous courtesans. From 1880 onwards, the capital owed to the fame of Montmartre a set of visitors of a more artistic kind, in flight from the boredom of England, as well as those of a more dissipated sort, fleeing from Victorian morality. This is a class of visitor frequently depicted in Lautrec's canvases: the English bon vivant, simultaneously impeccable and corrupt, a vicious bookmaker or a boxer turned milord. And yet his models were artists, living in Montmartre like himself and frequenting the same cafés.

A book had come out in 1888 called *Confessions of a Young Man*, which made Montmartre the capital of an Anglo-Saxon Bohemia. Its author, George Moore, an Anglo-Irishman of good family and some means, had come to Paris in 1873 with the intention of becoming a painter. The vulgarity which prevailed at the Ecole des Beaux-Arts sent him across the Seine. He shared a studio at the foot of the Butte with his friend Hawkins, who became a rather strange Symbolist painter. This Hawkins, who was English in name only, appears in the *Confessions* under the name of Marshall. A dandy and a seducer, he fascinated Moore, who was rather unattractive himself. Every night they would go up to the Moulin de la Galette or the Nouvelle Athènes and, as we have seen, Moore is still the best witness to the Montmartre of the Impressionists. Like them he can convey atmosphere to admiration without much regard for precise detail and he wrote:

> *Un pays ami* is truly a delicate delight – a country where we may go when daily life is becoming too daily, sure of finding there all the sensations of home plus those of irresponsible caprice. In Montmartre, I find a literature that is mine without being wholly mine, a literature that is like an exquisite mistress in whom I find consolation for all the commonplaces of life.

Zola and Manet were both friends of Moore and the latter painted a watercolour of the young man, who was also a client. They would all meet in a garden at Les Batignolles belonging to a *cocotte* married to a M. de Callias. Verlaine, Catulle Mendès, Villiers de l'Isle Adam, Mallarmé – reading Moore it sounds like a *fête champêtre* painted by Watteau. Other witnesses are not so sympathetic and it was rather rowdy. Moore, in this book and in his next, *Memories of a Dead Life*, describes some love affairs (imaginary, his friends said). It was an atmosphere of wit and a life devoted to art and to pleasure which could not be found in England, and from 1890 onwards there were a great many Englishmen in Montmartre, all, according to their means, endeavouring to reconstruct the collection of oddments Moore selected for his studio.

The best guide to the next generation is William Rothenstein. Coming from a Liverpool Jewish family, he was highly gifted with a pencil and a clever painter, but had been discouraged in his early artistic studies in London by the poor quality of the studios and by the lack of interest taken in young painters by the members of the Royal Academy. Rothenstein arrived in Paris in 1889, when he was seventeen, to work in the Académie Julian then in the Faubourg Saint-Denis. Famous Salon painters, such as Bouguereau and Benjamin Constant, supervised the work of students of every nationality. He met a young Australian painter, Charles Conder, who persuaded him to share his studio in Montmartre, in the Rue Ravignan, 'at the top of the street is an irregular open space bounded on the north by a flight of steps and railings, just below which are the studios. Above the steps was the pavilion of an eighteenth-century country house, beyond lie old, quiet streets, shuttered villas with deserted gardens and *terrains vagues*.' Conder hung the studio with eastern printed fabrics, spread Turkish cushions on the divans and entertained hordes of pretty girls, causing a constant interruption to the serious Rothenstein in his work. Conder already had a great many friends in Montmartre; he was often at the Moulin Rouge in company with Lautrec, who more than once put his white face with its shock of fair hair into one of his pictures, and with Anquetin, who, it was then thought, was going to become a great master. In between the absinths and the assignations, the young Australian painted ravishing fans on silk, part Japanese, part Whistler. Conder very quickly became a character in Montmartre and a guide for English newcomers. Oscar Wilde liked to meet him, very late at night, after dining in town, outside a café in the Place Pigalle. To impress him, Conder once stuck his companion's hat pin into his arm. 'How Baudelaire would have enjoyed that,' the poet remarked coolly. Wilde loved Conder's watercolours of crinolined ladies endeavouring to catch the Bluebird, and when they were exhibited, along with Rothenstein's drawings, in a little gallery in the Boulevard Malesherbes, he did his best to find purchasers for them, but as Wilde said with a sigh, 'Dear Conder! With what exquisite subtlety he goes about persuading someone to give him a hundred francs for a fan for which he was fully prepared to pay three hundred!' But even though amused by the passing of the male and female prostitutes in the boulevard, Wilde ultimately found the 'interminable *heure verte*' somewhat tedious, although he would have been very willing to become a peasant of Montmartre. Another Australian to join their circle was Phil May, a cartoonist not unlike Steinlen, who sent sketches of Montmartre to such magazines as the *Pick Me Up*. There was a splendid English girl, Sarah Brown, who fascinated these young men. She modelled for the most part for Rochegrosse but went now and then to the Académie Julian. Then her admirers would hasten down from Montmartre. She was the queen of the Bal des Quatzarts. One had to have seen her as Cleopatra, naked except for a golden net. All these young people, and Rothenstein mentions many who are now forgotten, had a huge admiration for Puvis de Chavannes, who could be seen at the same time every evening going up the Boulevard de Clichy, always on foot, on his way home from his distant studio in Neuilly. Albert Besnard once invited Rothenstein to lunch with Puvis. 'The great day arrived; but could this rubicund, large-nosed old gentleman, encased so correctly in a close-fitting frock coat, looking more like a senator than an artist, be Olympian Puvis?' The master's conversation was no more exciting than his appearance.

In spite of his bitterness and his prejudices, Degas was undoubtedly a more stimulating acquaintance for a young painter. He liked Rothenstein's drawings and opened his doors to him, as he had to Moore, and showed him in his turn his Ingres drawings and his latest pastels. He also welcomed another young Englishman, Walter Sickert. Through Degas, Sickert developed an awareness of the pictorial quality of the music halls, the artificial lights, tarnished gilding and slightly shopsoiled women. In 1898 he painted scenes from the music halls of Montmartre: the Eldorado, the Gaîté Rochechouart and the Théâtre Montmartre.

The other master who attracted the young English visitors, Gustave Moreau, lived right at the foot of Montmartre, in the Rue La Rochefoucauld, and never went up to the Butte. Wilde, who knew several of his admirers and loved his work, certainly visited the magician. It is much less likely that Beardsley, who owed so much to him, ever called on him; during his visits to Paris he went, first and foremost, to see Whistler on the left bank, but he enjoyed going to applaud Yvette Guilbert and sitting at café tables watching the girls go by. He was well acquainted with such journals as the *Courrier Français* and later on *Le Rire* and some of their illustrations, notably Vallotton's, had an influence on him. London in the nineties had a magazine that bore witness to this Parisian influence. The *Pick Me Up* followed in the footsteps of the *Chat Noir* and the *Mirliton* and its artists would imitate Steinlen or Vallotton. They included Raven Hill, Wright Manuel and Eckhardt, whose sketches drawn from life were the best advertisement for the pleasures of Montmartre. The articles, on the other hand, maintained a rather Victorian sententiousness, while at the same time giving a very accurate picture of what was to be found in divers establishments.

The little city on a hill wherein poverty breeds with discontent, where discontent breeds with crime, where crime ripens and putrifies into an ever new and powerful sore is a giant protest against the loveflushed capital below.

It's a bad quarter, Montmartre! Of the absinth drinker, hence the decadent. Of the idle and the vicious – hence the criminal Montmartre which never dreams but one dream, equality, and never grasps but one truth, reality.

That's the undercurrent!

Other, more disreputable Englishmen passed through Montmartre: Frank Harris, seeking love affairs, or Aleister Crowley, seeking esoteric cliques. The Americans came later and, in their hearts, always preferred the left bank. One, William Dannat, very gifted in a Sargentish way and much praised at the Salon, had a studio in the Boulevard de Clichy. Lorrain, who visited it, was amazed by a good taste which was in strong contrast to the junk that was the rule in other studios:

Oh, those vast, interconnecting ground floor rooms, decorated with such harmonious restraint, where the daylight, filtering through the frosted glass of the roof, falls grey and soft and even, eliminating the shadows of walls and corners. White woodwork and plain grey curtains, a carpet of the same soft grey on the floor, continuing through all the rooms, chairs and other furniture painted white. But on the walls the most vibrant and complementary colours furnished by a subtle selection of paintings, Raffaellis, Sargents, a Barrau and some canvases, at once delicate and dazzling, by the master of the house; here and there a few precious objects, but scattered, so that each has a decorative importance of its own, as for example, a Rodin in white marble standing all alone on the white-painted table in the salon.

The same Whistler-like tones were used again later by the American portrait painter, Romaine Brooks, when she had found herself a shabby apartment in the Boulevard de Clichy in order to get away from her mother. She tried modelling and then singing in a music hall, in the style of Jane Avril:

I agreed to dress up in a Kate Greenaway costume with a poke bonnet thrust over a wig of long yellow curls, and finally, with the 'Little Bit of String' as my sole repertoire, I was taken to a cabaret in a side street. There I made my *débuts*. The unusual get-up and awkward singing evidently went very well together, for I met with great success. But the shouting and stamping that went on even after I had left the stage was most alarming. It was all the more so when I understood that my audience was demanding that I dance a jig. I only knew the waltz, the polka, and other such conventional dances. Therefore, when the manager urged me to go back and dance '*n'importe quoi*', I firmly refused. It seemed to me an utterly impossible thing to do. The experience was horrible and for that very reason I forced myself to go through it several times. The greasy paints I plastered over my face, neck and arms; the queer cabotins and the pale, ill-looking manager who, to show his appreciation, would invite me to assist at the supper served on a long table to all the members of the cabaret.

Eckhardt: *An Englishman in Paris*. Drawing in the *Pick Me Up*, 1895

17
MOUNT CYTHERA

As we have just seen, the lax moral tone that prevailed in Montmartre did quite as much as the availability of teachers to keep Anglo-Saxon artists there. In its songs, its shows and its pictures, this *belle époque* seems to have a positive obsession with women, with the commercialization of women, and every quarter of Paris had its own, highly specialized style of prostitution. One has only to listen to the songs Bruant sang about Grenelle or the Bastille to realize that their ways were not those of Montmartre. For one thing, there were no brothels on the Butte itself. The cheap houses of ill-fame were to be found further east, in the direction of La Vilette, or westwards towards Clichy. The high-class establishments, like the one where Toulouse-Lautrec elected to live for several days, were round the Opéra. *Hôtels de passe*, on the other hand, were plentiful in the narrow streets leading up from the boulevard. There, the dalliance, although just as commercial, retained a semblance of spontaneity, with a stimulating game of courtships and assignations, and oglings at café tables. In short, the client could, at a price, get the illusion of being sought after. Nevertheless, the girls were *en carte*, that is subject to medical examinations and dependent on the goodwill of the police. Most of them made a pretence at some form of employment, either as dancers, or even singers, in the music halls, or, for the less dashing, passing as working girls, seamstresses, or, in the case of many of them, supposed milliners, even carrying professional pride to the lengths of going about with enormous hatboxes on their arms. There were pretended schoolgirls, accompanied by their mothers, real or assumed. The models were a class apart. The most expensive of these ladies could be encountered in the evenings, dressed up to the nines, at the Moulin Rouge or in the corridors of the Folies Bergère. A far cry from Gavarni's *grisettes*, they look very cynical as drawn by Forain, who was a frequent visitor to Montmartre round about 1880. They are the same silly, grasping creatures whom Degas studied at the Nouvelle Athènes. The remarks attributed to them by the cartoonists do not belie their looks; by 1880 they were adopting an artistic pose, with bandeaux and loose, flowing dresses. Then Forain gave up sharpening his teeth on such poor game and removed himself instead to the smart districts, savage, unkind but occasionally salutary.

The best painter of the girls of Montmartre was Bottini, a friend of Jean Lorrain's, who died very young of syphilis. Lorrain wrote a splendid introduction to the catalogue of his first exhibition:

It is the filth of Paris, its smoky air, heavy with fumes and vapours, which has wasted those pretty, pale nudes, eating their green apples. Yet there is also an innate elegance, a sumptuousness even, about the gestures and attitudes of these granddaughters of concierges; their doomed, theatrical beauty is the offence of Paris but it is also its glory and its crown. Little rats of the Opéra, lilies of the Rat Mort, *pierreuses* and *diamanteuses*, Bottini has outlined them all, ghostly girls against dark, rich grounds, shading from crimson lake to rusty red, backgrounds

Three prostitutes in bourgeois guise, about 1900

lifted here and there by touches of peacock blue and with a charm more imaginary than like anything seen in the real world, but with a use of colour both skilful and exciting.

Those colours, as though dark with age, were obtained by passing an iron over the gouaches. Bottini had started life as a faker and his work, for all its modernity, never lost something of the look of an old master. In a way Bottini was a little like a *fin de siècle* Constantin Guys. He has a kind of clumsiness which makes him more truthful than those other artists more influenced by Art Nouveau whose drawings of girls filled the magazines, for instance, Radiguet, Gerbault and, far better than either, Cappiello. It is well known what an influence they had on Picasso's early work.

There are a hundred novels, more or less pornographic, realistic or aesthetic, dealing with this side of Montmartre life, but no one has written about it with more

Toulouse-Lautrec: *Women in a brothel*, 1894. Albi, Musée Toulouse-Lautrec

(*right*) Toulouse-Lautrec: *Women in a brothel*, 1895. Budapest, Museum of Fine Arts

charm than Paul Léautaud in his novel *Le Petit Ami*, published in 1901:

It was at the top of the Rue Pigalle, not far from the Brasserie Fontaine, a kind of *crémerie*, now disappeared. Hardly anyone came there during the day. There, these women would lunch and dine together, lingering in the afternoon until it was time to go and dress, and in the evening until the time came to go and show themselves off in cafés or music halls, according to their assignations or their mood. . . . But for the most part we would go and spend the evening in various cafés or in places where there was music. I would sit with them, at a well-lit table, or we would stroll round the promenade together, they making eyes at all and sundry and I thinking of a thousand things. And from time to time one of them would leave us and go off to greet an old flame or another girl. At the end of the evening, supposing one of them had done no business and had an urge, not

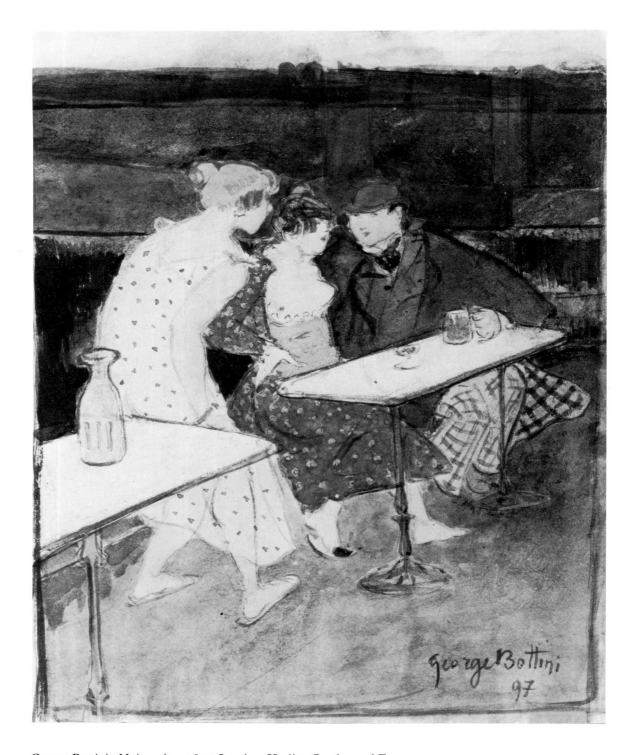

George Bottini: *Maison close*, 1897. London, Hazlitt, Gooden and Fox

too demanding, and the money for a cab, then I would accede readily to her proposal and go home with her.

By 1905, the motor car and the proliferation of electric signs of every colour were changing the atmosphere of the boulevard. It became a brilliant but also a sinister pleasure market which inspired Bonnard and Van Dongen on more than one occasion. A wealthier class of customer was invading Montmartre:

> The night clubs with their bright lights, shouting and laughter, gipsies and singers, never go to bed and fill the whole district with the noise of their revelry. Hordes of fiacres and motor taxis are parked or driving about, while policemen, armed with revolvers, order the confusion. Amid great swathes of light, the courtesans in huge hats and silken gowns move from door to door. The shapes of uniformed doormen loom up gigantically. Newsboys are busy trying to earn a few sous. And up the red-carpeted steps go the whole host of rollicking merrymakers and sad, restless night wanderers. (André Warnod)

Daragnes: *Girls at Pigalle*, about 1930

18
THE CIRCUS

Montmartre may be mystical or artistic but it is very seldom intellectual; its poets are the *chansonniers* and to the theatre it prefers the circus. There were lots of little theatres on the Butte; like the Atelier, which was built during the Restoration and, thanks to Charles Dullin, enjoyed a great period between the wars. But chiefly there were the music halls and the circus. The circus suited the rural side which Montmartre obstinately retained. It made one think of the travelling circuses which would set themselves up on the edge of a village and amaze the country people with their monsters, more or less genuine, their mangy wild beasts and assortment of acts. The Cirque Fernando was on a fixed site, it is true, although it retained the shape of a circular tent, built of wood painted in garish colours, and the attractions were of the highest order, but it did stand on the outskirts of the village, on the far side of the Boulevard Rochechouart, and it was highly popular with all who loved the action, the finery and the fanfares and whose admiration was given more to physical than to mental agility.

The Cirque Fernando was famous above all for its horse-riding acts, which, beautiful as they are, strike us today as slightly monotonous. But then nearly everyone prided themselves on a knowledge of horses, and furthermore the equestriennes, with their boots and their whips, excited a certain kind of audience. Among those to be seen there was Ada Menken, who was said to have had an affair with the Empress of Austria, herself a passionate admirer of *haute école*. Lautrec was very much aware of this disturbing woman/horse relationship. He, who saw human beings only as caricatures, gave the horses a great style which contrasts with the hard, ambiguous look of the rider, with her painted face and her tutu, like the dancer on horseback in the celebrated picture in the Chicago Museum, the *Ecuyère du Cirque Fernando*.

If certain men with masochistic tendencies were excited by the equestriennes, women with sadistic leanings waited for one of the handsome trapeze artistes to fall. One of Jean Lorrain's heroines, called, untranslatably, *la pompe funèbre*, drained the young acrobats before they were even on.

An acrobat, his spangled nakedness gleaming fitfully with sweat and the electric lights, threw himself backwards with an arching of his whole body and then, drawing himself up suddenly, straightening his hips and pointing his legs skywards, treated them to the magical vision of a man become all rhythm, a supple swinging like the movement of a fan. 'Confess that you almost long for him to fall. Indeed, I do myself, and there are lots of people here in the same state of dreadful expectation. It is the horrible instinct of the crowd in the face of something which rouses it to thoughts of lust and death.'

Two clowns who made a great hit at that time were Footit and Chocolat. Lautrec painted them many times. There was also a big woman, half-clown and half-equestrienne, called Cha-U-Kao, who was a familiar figure at the Moulin Rouge.

Toulouse-Lautrec: *Cha-U-Kao*. Lithograph, 1896

AU CIRQUE FERNANDO, — par HENRIOT.

SAUTS DU CLOWN GASSION
Plus rapide que le téléphone.

Un cheval à qui M. Frederichs essaye de monter le cou.

LE SINGE PIERROT et le CHEVAL BÉBÉ.

PACHA, CHEVAL RAPPORTEUR.
Évidemment, puisqu'il rapporte énormément à M. L. Fernando.

L'ÉCHELLE D'ARGENT.
(Mlle Élize et M. Williams.)
Échelle que ne monterait pas le budget.

Mlle JUTELAIS, jongleries et équilibres.
Si légère qu'on ne sait si elle supporte le fil, ou si le fil la supporte.

C. W. FISCH, champion américain.
Hip hip! hourra!...
Pour faire des sauts périlleux à cheval, en voilà u qui s'en fiche!

The attractions of the Cirque Fernando in 1886 by Henriot

(*left*) Poster for the Cirque Fernando, about 1880

Degas, too, was a frequent visitor to the circus. In 1879 he painted one of his most famous pictures: Mlle La La, trapeze artiste at the Cirque Fernando, hanging by her teeth from an iron ring in the orange light of the gas lamps. He loved to see just how disjointed the female animal could become. Renoir, on the other hand, saw two little girl jugglers, who do not seem to know quite what to do with their oranges, above all as an enchanting theme in the gay colours that belong to the circus. Another regular visitor to the Cirque Fernando was Seurat. His last studio was not far away in the Passage de l'Elysée des Beaux-Arts. He was thrilled by the equestriennes and the clowns and tried, through them, to convey the sense of movement. One of the clowns from the Cirque Fernando, Clovis Sagot, became a picture dealer – he knew so many painters. Later on, Picasso, too, went to the Montmartre circus and treated the turns he saw there more poetically because of his memories of the wretched companies that toured Spain, graceful, desperate mountebanks, objects of envy to all those doomed to eke out a dreary existence.

The Cirque Fernando was pulled down in 1900 and rebuilt in a more permanent form, to survive until the present day under the name of the Cirque Medrano. There one could see the famous clowns, the Fratellinis, and the acrobatic turn which so fascinated Jean Cocteau: Barbette, an American young man of remarkable good looks and muscles of steel, who would swing from one trapeze to another, dressed in gowns from the greatest couturiers, and who invented a kind of strip-tease on the slack wire.

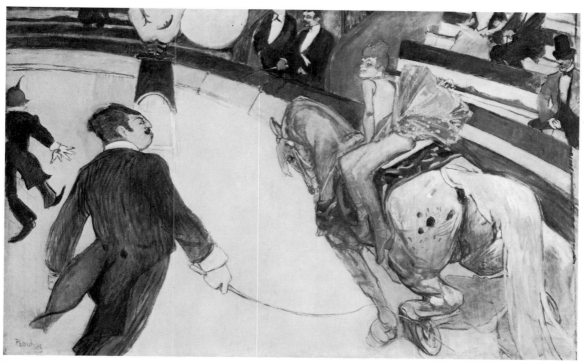

Toulouse-Lautrec: *In the Cirque Fernando: the ringmaster*, 1888. Chicago, Art Institute

(*left*) Toulouse-Lautrec: *The flying trapeze*, 1899. Cambridge, Mass., Fogg Art Museum

Toulouse-Lautrec: *Chocolat dancing*, 1896. Albi, Musée Toulouse-Lautrec

(*left*) Footit and Chocolat, the famous clowns from the Cirque Fernando whom Toulouse-Lautrec often sketched

There were circus turns at the Moulin Rouge as well, and at the Folies Bergère and, twice a year, when the middle of the Boulevard Rochechouart was taken over by a fair, in between the roundabouts and the stalls selling sticky sweets, the boxers would set up their booths. In the days before boxing became a world sport, pugilists were a fairground attraction for amateurs to try their skill against. Here, too, on a lower level, the atmosphere was distinctly fraught. Elderly gentlemen would be there feeling the muscles of the young amateurs, on the excuse that they were keen on

(*right*) Poster by Orazy for the Hippodrome. Chariot races in the classical style were held there, but the drivers were women not men

The Hippodrome built on the Boulevard de Clichy in 1895

encouraging the sport. Jean Lorrain, who had a weakness for boxers in flesh-pink vests and tigerskin shorts, was great friends with the most famous of them, Toulouse, and he arranged for some of his female friends to make the acquaintance of Toulouse's most promising young men, reserving to himself the right to make fun of them when they ventured into disreputable haunts to get a closer view of their prospective conquests.

> On Thursday evening she was at the Casino de Paris, her eyes riveted keenly on the sweat-soaked vests of Tom Cannon and Pons: green underneath her rouge, pale as a rotting corpse and her lips set in a nervous smile, she was there again yesterday at the bout between Pons and the Greek, Pieri, her eyes fixed, claw-like, on the swelling pectoral muscles and bunched biceps of the two rival champions!

Montmartre had another circus, but this one was a vast hippodrome near the Place Clichy, an imitation of the Roman circuses. Chariot races were put on there, the drivers being girls with helmets and flying hair who looked more like Valkyries than charioteers. These shows were very expensive and in about 1900 Hornbeck's menagerie found a home in the hippodrome. Ten years after that the Gaumont Cinema Corporation built the biggest cinema in the world on the site, showing the films of Max Linder, who now and then foreshadowed Charlie Chaplin.

The proximity of the Cirque Fernando and the music halls made Montmartre a centre for recruiting circus artistes. In between engagements, trapeze artistes, conjurors, equestriennes and clowns lived in the small hotels, not all of them of ill repute, around the Place Blanche. It was there that Severini got to know a troupe of trapeze artistes. He would go and watch them practising in the mornings and at night to see the dazzling shimmer of spangled tights high above the ring. That and the crowd scattered like a handful of confetti on the tiered benches had a great influence on the development of Divisionism.

When Diaghilev put on the ballet *Parade* in 1917, Picasso's sets as well as Satie's music were reminiscent of the circuses that used to go up twice a year in the Boulevard Rochechouart.

The last appearance of the circus and the fairground booths of Montmartre was in 1945, with that fine ballet *Les Forains* set to music by Henry Sauguet and with costumes by Christian Berard. It conveyed very well the melancholy, ephemeral beauty of the 'Picasso blue period' side to the mountebanks, putting up their makeshift stages for indifferent audiences and then packing up again to take their poverty and their dreams on somewhere else.

Renoir: *Circus girls*, 1879. Chicago, Art Institute

Seurat: *Cirque*, 1890–1. Paris, Louvre

(*left*) Degas: *La La at the Cirque Fernando*, 1879. London, National Gallery

19
THE BATEAU~LAVOIR

On a hot May day in 1907, two American ladies, one large and clad in the vaguely classical draperies made fashionable by Isadora Duncan and the other small and dark, with something of the look of an out-of-work Spanish dancer, left their flat near the Luxembourg to go to Montmartre, which, at that time, was a real expedition. But suppose we listen to Miss Stein, speaking through the lips of Miss Toklas:

> We went to the Odeon and there got into an omnibus, that is we mounted on top of an omnibus, the nice old horse-pulled omnibuses that went pretty quickly and steadily across Paris and up the hill to the Place Blanche. There we got out and climbed a steep street lined with shops with things to eat, the Rue Lepic, and then turning we went around a corner and climbed even more steeply in fact almost straight up and came to the Rue Ravignan, now Place Emile-Goudeau but otherwise unchanged, with its steps leading up to the little flat square with its few but tender little trees, a man carpentering in the corner of it, the last time I was there not very long ago there was still a man carpentering in a corner of it, and a little café just before you went up the steps where they all used to eat, it is still there, and to the left a low wooden building of studios that is still there.
>
> We went up the couple of steps and through the open door passing on our left the studio in which later Juan Gris was to live out his martyrdom but where there lived a certain Vaillant, a nondescript painter who was to lend his studio as a ladies dressing room at the famous banquet for Rousseau, and then we passed a steep flight of steps leading down where Max Jacob had a studio a little later, and we passed another steep little stairway which led to the studio where not long before a young fellow had committed suicide, Picasso painted one of the most wonderful of his early pictures of the friends gathered round the coffin, we passed all this to a larger door where Gertrude Stein knocked and Picasso opened the door and we went in. (*The Autobiography of Alice B. Toklas*)

This block of studios, originally intended for artisans and not for artists, had been called, for no very obvious reason, La Maison du Castor; the name Bateau-Lavoir probably arose from the way the womenfolk of the painters who began moving in there round about 1890 used to hang their washing across from one window to another. The entrance was by a little door in the Place Ravignan, now Emile-Goudeau. A few trees, one pretentious block of flats and the Hôtel du Poirier made up the rest of the little square, where on summer evenings people would gather to take the air and gossip around the Wallace fountain. Once inside the door, you went down instead of up; the huge building, with walls made of brick and timber pierced by enormous lights, was on four floors built against the side of the Butte, facing a narrow courtyard flanked on its other side by a blackened retaining wall; in the courtyard was a single tap for all the tenants. It was pervaded by a strong smell of cockroaches and, on some summer days, of disinfectant. Evidence of poverty was everywhere, but of the dilapidated rather than the picturesque variety. The

Painting by Marie Laurençin of Apollinaire, Picasso and herself

condition of the studios had gone downhill since Rothenstein and Conder had shared one fifteen years earlier. But the rent was only fifteen francs a month, whereas a room at the Hôtel du Poirier cost one franc a night. The ground floor was occupied by a puppet master who would wake the tenants every morning with a roll of drums.

From 1903, the most colourful and popular of the Bateau-Lavoir's tenants was Picasso. He had arrived in Paris in April 1901 with a friend and, drawn by the reputation of Montmartre and kept there by its cheapness, they had shared a room at 130 Boulevard de Clichy. At once the artist who signed his rather Pre-Raphaelitish pictures with the name Pablo Ruiz Picasso threw himself into the Montmartre of Toulouse-Lautrec. He pinned up the poster of May Milton on his wall. From his very first canvases, his world became the world of Montmartre: a Moulin de la Galette, a view plunging steeply down to the Boulevard de Clichy, the fair in the Boulevard Rochechouart, exotically dressed women glimpsed through the windows of expensive restaurants. He was lucky enough to be able to exhibit all this at the Galerie Vollard, slipping into the exhibition of a Basque friend, Iturrino, who lived in Montmartre for many years and posed for the Belgian painter Evenepoel in front of the Moulin Rouge, a picture which was famous at the time.

In the streets, Picasso recognized the models for the work of Steinlen, which he knew very well from the illustrated papers which used to reach Barcelona. Until that time artists had painted the poor as either resigned or picturesque; Picasso, in his Blue Period, followed Steinlen and drew the poor as erotic. Puvis de Chavannes, in *The Poor Fisherman* and *The Prodigal Son*, had already treated poverty with a dignity wholly devoid of the picturesque. Picasso, who was a great admirer of Puvis, gave it charm. Another Spanish artist, named Zuloaga, very nearly forgotten today but who was then beginning to acquire a considerable reputation, also lived in Montmartre and was always glad to see his fellow countrymen. Zuloaga was a bit of a Velazquez of Montmartre, painting the damsels of the *maisons closes*, except when the Butte, seen in the background of his portraits, began to look like El Greco's Toledo. He painted *demi-mondaines* before he painted infantas. There were a great many Spaniards in Montmartre and this was why Picasso, who spent his time surrounded by his fellow countrymen, took so long to learn French. Picasso very soon quarrelled with the friend who shared his room because he would bring friends home every evening and spend the night in talk, their endless *tertullias*; and so he went back to Barcelona.

During this first stay in Paris, Picasso made one very good friend who took him in when he returned some months later. This was Max Jacob, who had admired the work he showed at Vollard's. At twenty-six, ugly and homosexual, Max for the first time found himself warmly welcomed by these Spaniards. He was in love with Picasso and wrote about him: 'He was perfectly beautiful, a face like ivory, without a wrinkle, in which his eyes shone much larger than today, and the crow's wing of his hair over a little forehead like a casket. . . . I believed in him more than in myself.'

On his return, Max Jacob offered Picasso a bed in his gloomy flat in the Boulevard

Barbès, then, when Picasso moved into the Bateau-Lavoir, where his friend the sculptor Paco Durio was living, Max lived for some years in the Rue Ravignan and became, with his monocle and his bowler hat, one of the characters of the Butte.

After he moved into Paco Durio's studio, Picasso lost no time in installing a beautiful girl there, Fernande Olivier. She was a girl of the working class and after an unhappy marriage she had taken to living among the painters, passing from one to another. This is how Fernande described the studio where the masterpieces of the Blue Period were painted, in which her own slanting eyes and long, thin mouth are often to be seen:

> A mattress on four legs in one corner. A little rusty cast-iron stove with a yellow earthenware bowl on it which was used for washing; a towel and a piece of soap were on a white wooden table next to it. In another corner, a poor little black painted trunk made a rather uncomfortable seat. A wicker chair, easels, canvases of all sizes, tubes of paint scattered about the floor . . . no curtains! In the table drawer there was a tame white mouse, which Picasso looked after lovingly and would show to everybody.   (*Picasso and his Friends*)

Someone with a sense of humour had hung a chart of foreign coinage on the wall above the bed; the studio was heated by the wretched cast-iron stove on which the cooking was done. Round this stove, on the bed or on the floor, friends would gather on most evenings, bringing a sausage or a bottle of red wine, and arguing endlessly about painting. One, called Piaget, now forgotten, laid down the principles of what was very soon to become Cubism. If Max was there, he would dominate the conversation with a mixture of intelligence and extreme eccentricity, coupled with great strictures on all the various kinds of bad taste which flourished on the Butte. On such evenings, Picasso would say to him: 'Max, let's do Degas,' and then nothing was spared their wit. On really bad days, Max would launch into wild improvisations.

> No one had the six sous for a beer across the road and, under the zinc-shaded paraffin lamp hanging by a wire hook from the cobwebby beams, we made up whole scenes, and crazy charades. There was the funeral of Sarah Bernhardt (still very much alive), and the Prompter and the Prima Donna (a tragedy). Picasso would laugh and take part, and his laughter was our object. (Max Jacob)

Yes, Max was indispensable to the Bateau-Lavoir. He succeeded in selling articles in praise of his friend to the little reviews. He discovered a secondhand dealer in the Rue des Martyrs, Père Soulier, who would buy Picasso's drawings for anything from fifty centimes to two francs according to size, drawings which would fall from him as easily as leaves from a tree while he was painting the Harlequins and acrobats or practising engraving. Quite frequently, Picasso and Fernande would go to the cinematograph in the Rue de Douai or else to the Cirque Medrano.

Max disliked Fernande, who was very bohemian and lazy and made no effort to make life more comfortable. For example, as soon as they had any money they would go to a restaurant and then linger late into the night in the cabarets where they could always be sure of meeting friends. Their favourite haunt was Frédé's, the Lapin Agile. We shall see a little further on what this high spot of bohemianism was like; it was ruled by a spirit of practical jokery, which reached its peak with the banquet put on at the Bateau-Lavoir in the spring of 1908 in honour of Le Douanier Rousseau and organized by Guillaume Apollinaire and a number of other young poets, partly as a joke against the old primitive. There were paper lanterns and streamers saying *'Honneur à Rousseau'*. The walls were decked with garlands of paper flowers. There was a great deal of singing and Apollinaire made up a poem on the spur of the moment:

> *Tu te souviens, Rousseau, du paysage aztèque,*
> *Des forêts où poussaient la mangue et l'ananas . . .*

> Rousseau, do you recall that Aztec scene,
> Jungles where mangoes and pineapples grew . . .

This was because Rousseau had taken part in Napoleon III's Mexican campaign. Marie Laurencin sang some romantic songs, drank two glasses of wine and collapsed

Picasso's rent receipt for the Bateau-Lavoir

(*right*) Photograph of Picasso in 1904

À mes chers amis
Suzanne et Henri
Picasso
1904

Bibi la Purée, a celebrity in the Montmartre cabarets of the nineties. La Purée is slang for poverty

into a corner. She did not care for Fernande and liked to play the well brought up young lady, although she had grown up in the Boulevard de la Chapelle. The Douanier, moved to tears, told Picasso: 'We are the two greatest painters of the age, you in the Egyptian style and I in the modern.'

From this rowdy evening, Picasso acquired rather a bad reputation. He was beginning to have had enough of having his studio cluttered with friends, and friends' friends and friends' friends' girlfriends. Fernande was quite happy amid all the confusion but he tired of it, and very soon of Fernande. In his heart, he much preferred hard work to bohemianism. He had got to know some more serious people, Braque and Matisse, hardworking bourgeois. His pictures were beginning to sell quite well, so he left the Bateau-Lavoir and the Rue Ravignan for a nice flat in the Boulevard de Clichy, a middle-class apartment which required proper furniture and had a large studio. When he entertained his guests were served by a maid in a white apron. These friends were Juan Gris, the dealer Kahnweiler, Marcoussis, and the girlfriend who very soon came to replace Fernande.

The Bateau-Lavoir had other tenants who also became famous: Juan Gris and for several years Van Dongen. He came from Rotterdam on an excursion ticket at the age of eighteen. He promptly threw away the return half and hastened to Montmartre. He was a handsome boy and the girls took pity on him so that he managed not to starve before the magazines started accepting his drawings. Van Dongen moved into the Bateau-Lavoir in 1900 and lived a more bourgeois life than Picasso with a model by whom he had a little girl. Picasso used to make rag dolls for her and paint them. All the same, there was no great sympathy between the Spaniard and the Dutchman who had no particular intellectual bent and preferred to spend his evenings sketching at the Moulin Rouge or the Bal Tabarin. But he did attract his friends Derain and Vlaminck to Montmartre. In 1908 Derain had a gloomy studio in the Villa des Fusains, in the Rue Tourlaque, a kind of junk shop crammed with his finds from the Flea Market. Vlaminck was on friendly terms with anarchists who met at the journal *Le Libertaire*'s offices in the Rue d'Orsel. But the Fauves enjoyed life too much to be really happy in the mournful atmosphere of the Bateau-Lavoir, for even the better type of these Montmartre studios often had their tragic moments. André Warnod, who was the best observer of the Butte prior to 1914, wrote:

> In the studios, the twilight falls slowly through the high windows like an imperceptible grey ash, enveloping and attenuating the forms of things. The dimness fills with mystery, a faint unease has come with the evening; the girl who is there, pressed close like some tiny creature, is not always the one you would wish for and, slowly, you sink into an infinite depression, without the strength to tear yourself away and go in search of the bright lights.

When the *cafard* was aggravated by poverty and drugs, the outcome was suicide. There were several at the Bateau-Lavoir. The most celebrated, if one can call it that,

was when a German painter, Vigels, very handsome and heavily drugged, hanged himself. The funeral procession set out from the Bateau-Lavoir with Père Frédé, proprietor of the Lapin Agile, at its head, followed by a crowd of art students dressed in brightly coloured finery because the dead man had used a palette full of colours in his work. Out of the windows of a fiacre, drunken girls waved to passers-by as they took their hats off to the hearse. A tramp, called Bibi la Purée, a shoeblack and a great talker, brought up the rear, dressed in a morning coat. He laid claim to be a poet, had known Verlaine and is remembered because Picasso and Jacques Villon painted him.

We can understand why Picasso left the Bateau-Lavoir as soon as he had some money; what remains of those years is the Blue Period. But he kept a studio there, where, in 1910, he used to meet Marcelle, friend of Marcoussis, one of the first Cubists. And long afterwards he still had a nostalgia for that impoverished period when he first realized his genius. Van Dongen, too, retained no bad memories of those grim studios, since he gave the name Bateau-Lavoir to the luxurious villa he built thirty years later on the Côte d'Azur.

Henri Evenepoel: *The Spaniard in Paris*, 1899. Musée des Beaux-Arts, Ghent

20

THE LAPIN AGILE

Picasso's fame has rubbed off on the sordid places where his genius developed. In some biographies, the Bateau-Lavoir becomes a sort of Bethlehem stable and the cabaret of the Lapin Agile, where the painter spent many evenings, takes on, for some, the dignity of Plato's Academy. But if this establishment was the haunt of a whole generation of young people who attained to some degree of fame, it may be said that Picasso was far from going there every night and that more often than not it was Fernande who took him there. Remember that although Max Jacob and Guillaume Apollinaire might enjoy the jokes that were got up there under the aegis of Père Frédé, they always refused to recite their verses in between the songs.

During the Second Empire there was a wretched little *guinguette* on the corner of the Rue Saint-Vincent with a little terrace looking out over the northern suburb. It was called the Cabaret des Assassins, as much because of its customers as on account of the murals depicting the many crimes of Troppmann, for which he was executed in 1869, which decorated the walls. After the Commune, the caricaturist Gill painted a sign for this cabaret, of a rabbit jumping into a pot, which was also a pun on the artist's name – the *lapin à Gill*, or the *lapin agile*. In 1903 the proprietor was Père Frédé, who, for thirty years, was one of the most famous characters on the Butte, with his grizzled beard, long hair worn under a fur hat, sweater and boots.

Frédé had previously kept a little cabaret called Le Zut, where Picasso used to meet his friends during his first visit to Paris. It may have been that the bareness of the place reminded the Spaniards of their own village taverns. To make themselves feel still more at home, they whitewashed the walls and one night, while drinking sangria, Picasso painted an impromptu Temptation of St Anthony.

Frédé would play the guitar and sing sentimental ballads or drinking songs. He was a born host, on familiar terms with everyone on sight, making one recite, another sing, leading the applause and passing round the hat, as well as keeping an eye on his daughter, who waited on the customers. He used to declare that the first duty of an artist was to have a good digestion, and it certainly needed one to swallow his special cocktail, a mixture of pernod and grenadine. Just as in other cabarets, the walls were covered with works of art, the red-shaded lamps throwing a sinister glow over them. A larger than life and excessively realistic Christ Crucified dominated the room, in between the casts of Apollo Musagetes and a Hindu god. Then there was Picasso's picture *Arlequin et sa Compagne*, which Frédé later sold to the Swedish choreographer Rolph de Mares, some Utrillos, some drawings by Steinlen, and various daubs whose fame never spread beyond Montmartre, or lasted more than a single season. The customers were made to write a poem each and there are verses by André Salmon and Jehan Rictus, alongside the signatures of Clemenceau, Renoir, Forain and Léon Bloy. . . . There were also some less desirable characters, and one night Frédé's son was stabbed in a brawl. His daughter, Margot, finally married the novelist Mac Orlan, but that was long after Picasso painted her, with a tame crow on her shoulder.

Frédé entertaining François Poulbot, the painter, and his friends at the Lapin Agile in 1905

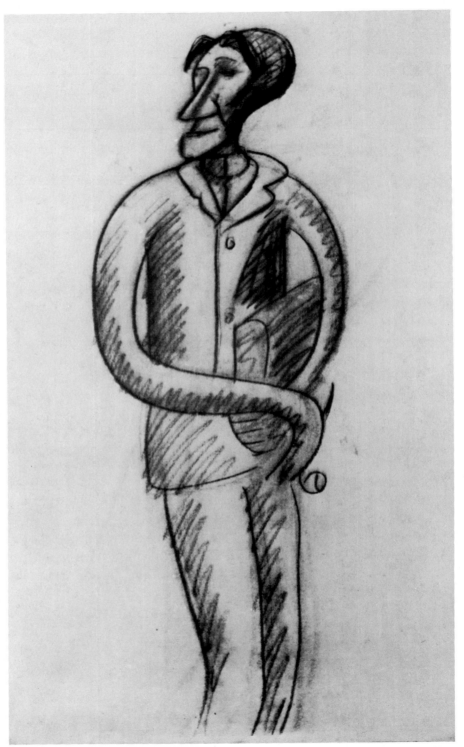

Portrait of André Salmon by Picasso. Salmon was, with Apollinaire, one of the first critics of Cubism

(*right*) Bonnard: *Boulevard des Batignolles*, 1907. Paris, Private Collection

There was generally a donkey tied up at the door of the cabaret and this animal had its hour of fame. The young art students who frequented the Lapin Agile put it about that a certain Raphael Boronali, creator of the Excessivist school, whose manifesto was remarkably like that of the Futurists, was going to exhibit at the Salon d'Automne. What they had done was to fasten a paintbrush to the donkey's tail, then dip it into pots of paint and let him swish it over a canvas, calling the result *Sunset over the Adriatic*. They fed the donkey with carrots to encourage him to swish his tail more vigorously. The work attracted a great deal of notice at the autumn Salon of 1912 and sold for four hundred francs.

Every year, the Salon d'Automne drew the painters of Montmartre down to the Grand Palais in the Champs-Elysées, where every kind of innovation was welcomed. After the opening ceremony, the painters would pile into cars and fiacres to go back up to the Place du Tertre to celebrate their successes at Frédé's. By this time he had been obliged to move out of the old Lapin Agile because it was no longer big enough. By about 1905 or 1906 the reputation of the Lapin Agile as a centre of all things *avant-garde* was well established. The more inquisitive art critics would venture there, like Wilhelm Uhde, who did so much to make Picasso known. A photograph taken at Frédé's on a holiday shows him surrounded by his regular customers. Among those present are Fernande, Apollinaire, the composer Gustave Charpentier, and two young writers who used themes associated with Montmartre all their lives, Francis Carco and Roland Dorgelès. Besides these, there are a horde of '*artistes*', which means anyone with artistic leanings and more ideas than practical technique. The '*artiste*' had to be self-taught, or at least have forgotten everything he was taught, but he had to have the artistic temperament. The idea of exhibiting the work of painters wholly ignorant of their trade took on very quickly. Workers disillusioned with anarchy, bourgeois with an aversion to work, rich boys come down in the world, they all became '*artistes*'. Their style of dress, popularized by the illustrated papers, became like the Breton shepherds or Louis XV courtiers to be seen at fancy dress balls. They were credited with extraordinary love affairs and a talent for practical jokes.

Modigliani, the reserved and shabby dandy who arrived in Montmartre in 1905 and immediately found his way to the Lapin Agile was no more an '*artiste*' than Picasso. The two painters did not take to one another. Picasso's working-class clothes seemed to Modigliani an affectation, while Picasso said of him: 'You never see him drunk except somewhere he can cause trouble.' A shed in the Rue Lepic served the young Italian as a studio. For a time he shared an abandoned shack called the Maison du Curé with another painter, Gaston Modot. But for the most part he slept in the Rue Norvins with his mistress, an English poetess called Beatrice Hastings. At heart, Modigliani preferred hashish to alcohol: some houses in the Maquis were real opium dens. After his meeting with a young picture dealer, Paul Guillaume, in 1912, Modigliani had more money and painted his monotonous nudes,

Bonnard: *Place Clichy*, 1912. Paris, Private Collection

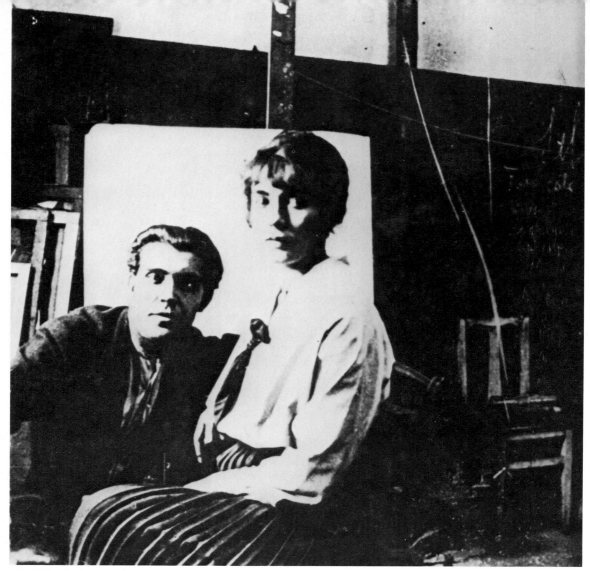

Modigliani, about 1912

which are so easily forged. It was not long before he departed for Montparnasse.

Modigliani had introduced the Futurists to Montmartre. The most famous of them, and the noisiest, Marinetti, did not stay because everyone there was poor, but the most attractive, Severini, remained there until 1917. Boccioni, too, stayed for two years. These Italians went a great deal to the Lapin Agile but also to the Café de l'Hermitage in the Boulevard de Clichy. Encouraged by Félix Fénéon, Severini carried Signac's experiments a stage further, resulting in the Divisionists. The atmosphere of the Montmartre dance halls, with their garish colours, bright lights and whirling dancers inspired several of his paintings, the largest of which is *Pan Pan à Monico* (*opposite page 191*). His studio was in a brand-new block in the Impasse de Guelma off the Boulevard Rochechouart. Braque and Dufy had their studios there for a time but they can scarcely be counted among the characters of Montmartre. They were hardly ever seen at the Lapin Agile.

Picasso left Montmartre in 1912. His big flat in the Boulevard de Clichy was still too easily accessible to his bohemian friends, who had ceased to amuse him and only wasted his time. He crossed the Seine and went to live in the Boulevard Raspail, near Montparnasse, not far from the Rue de Fleurus, where the Steins lived. His departure marks the decline of Montmartre as an artistic centre. And so, after the war, when the fame of the Lapin Agile had spread world-wide, there was only a token band of art students and tourists to listen to Père Frédé's songs. The '*artistes*' begrudged the success of their elders. They would write in large letters on the walls: 'Matisse sends you mad' and 'Matisse is more dangerous than absinth'. In Frédé's golden book, the sketch that he would show most proudly was a drawing of a shoe done by Charlie Chaplin during a visit to Montmartre.

Rue des Saules. The Lapin Agile, also known as the Cabaret des Assassins, about 1900

21
THE BOULEVARDS OF SODOM

Montmartre has a place apart, almost a sacred place in the annals of pederasty. It was on the Butte, indeed, that Verlaine first met Arthur Rimbaud, come from Charleville in answer to that most celebrated letter: '*Venez chère âme, on vous attend, on vous désire.*' Verlaine was not long married and Madame Verlaine's brother, the musician, Charles de Sivery, would try to smooth matters over whenever the poet came home too drunk, but Sivery gave up trying to make the peace when Verlaine introduced into his house a provincial admirer who had written to him and who eventually became his lover, the eighteen-year-old poet Arthur Rimbaud. Forain, a close friend of Rimbaud's, was involved in many of the dramas which attended the affair between the two poets. Although Verlaine and Rimbaud spent little time in Montmartre after this first meeting, they had their effect on the spirit of Montmartre. In this spirit, piety and debauchery lived side by side, everything ended in heaven for the admirers of Verlaine and in hell for those of Rimbaud.

Jean Lorrain, again, in a poem in his first collection, *Modernités*, wrote of the boys strolling up and down on the look-out for clients. He had a weakness for the boxers who would put up their booths at the fair in the Boulevard Rochechouart.

> Those gentlemen of the ring, a tiger skin
> About their loins, bare chests, their own skins firm and clear.

He boasted that, in his own words: '*J'ai couché cette nuit entre deux débardeurs, ils m'ont débarassé de toutes mes ardeurs.*' One section of the book is called *Fleurs de Boue*. In those days it took a certain amount of courage to celebrate such dealings, even in verse. Certainly the Boulevard de Clichy soon had an unsavoury reputation. Those broad, ill-lit avenues, planted down the middle with plane trees and with a urinal every hundred yards or so, known delicately as an *édifice Rambuteau* after the prefect of police under Louis-Philippe, lent themselves perfectly to the hide-and-seek of every kind of prostitution. The fairs that filled the boulevard twice yearly were also a convenient place for pick-ups, in the flickering light of the paraffin lamps.

After all, Toulouse-Lautrec painted Oscar Wilde outside the booth of La Goulue, probably more interested in some youths than in the one-time star of the Moulin Rouge. When he went to hear Jehan Rictus, Wilde was delighted with the young doorman who asked for his autograph: 'I've already got fifty-three poets and two musicians in my book.' During his first stay in Paris, Wilde had ventured into the Château Rouge, where his kind were far from welcome. When some of the young men began eyeing the table where he was sitting with his friend Sherard in a threatening way, Sherard, not the brightest of men, told them: 'The first man who dares to attack my friend Monsieur Oscar Wilde will have me to deal with.' 'Robert,' said Oscar gently, 'you are defending me at the risk of my life.'

An extremely obscene novel called *Teleny*, published in the late nineties, was attributed to Wilde but was more probably written by one of his young friends

Bottini: *The wrestlers of the Boulevard de Clichy*

Oscar Wilde outside La Goulue's booth (*see page 72*)

because it contains some of the poet's fantasies but none of his wit. One passage from this book gives a vivid description of the homosexual world of the boulevards.

> He lingered once more, let me pass, walked on at a brisker pace, and was again beside me. Finally, I looked at him. Though it was cold, he was but slightly dressed. He wore a short, black velvet jacket and a pair of light grey, closely-fitting trousers marking the shape of the thighs and buttocks like tights. As I looked at him he stared at me again, then smiled with that vacant, vapid, idiotic facial contraction of a *raccrocheuse*. Then, always looking at me with an inviting leer, he directed his steps towards a neighbouring Vespasienne. . . .
>
> After a while I again heard steps coming from behind; the person was close up to me. I smelt a strong scent – if the noxious odour of musk or of patchouli can be called a scent.
>
> His eyes were painted with kohl, his cheeks were dabbed with rouge. He was quite beardless. For a moment I doubted whether he was a man or a woman; but when he stopped again before the column I was fully persuaded of his sex. Someone else came with mincing steps, and shaking his buttocks, from behind one of these pissoirs. He was an old, wiry, simpering man, as shrivelled as a frostbitten pippin. His cheeks were very hollow and his projecting cheek bones very red; his face was shaven and shorn, and he wore long, fair, flaxen locks.

We find the same people some twenty years later in Francis Carco's novel *Jésus la Caille*. (A *jésus* in argot is a pretty, effeminate boy.) This is the best novel of the Montmartre that trades in every kind of love, the masterpiece of the *nostalgie de la boue*. The rain on the boulevards, where the girls have young men as their rivals, the whine of the gramophones in the bars, the dawn tarnishing the brightness of the lights in cafés where the customers still have not made up their minds about a partner, the hotels with their dirty flowered wallpaper where they sleep until two in the afternoon, the accordionists at the street corners. All this picturesque melancholy, so familiar to us from the cinema, becomes, with Carco, a part of literature. After the Bohemia launched by the Goncourts fifty years before, now it was the turn of the *canaille*. Suppose we follow Carco into the Bar de la Palme in the Boulevard de Clichy: the prostitute, Fernande, falls in love with Jésus la Caille:

> At the next table she noticed, in the pallor that emphasized the warm brown of his eyelids and the bloom on his lips, an exhausted wastrel, funny and delicate. A friend confides to her: 'That Jésus is more gorgeous than a girl.' A go-between is offering two little working boys, Pompon and Lolotte, to her clients: 'I've two fine lads, messieurs.'

Let us go with Carco into another curious establishment:

> In the little bar on the first floor the most peculiar art lover was admiring some photographic prints. Bousse possessed some curious series and in that way he

found, right in the middle of Montmartre, a façade roughly whitewashed over a thousand times. The bar led to the salon. The salon gave on to the hall. A variety of little studios, very well furnished, were there for the reception of the connoisseurs, who could ask for a reconstruction of any subject of their choice. The art lover requested the Three Graces and shut himself in with them, even though the group was posed by models of a different sex from the original. From the very first day, Jésus la Caille's Medici Venus made his reputation.

For those who were not particularly keen on young boys, there were a good many so-called sailors strolling in the Place Pigalle. The police had to restore order there after a number of brawls. The pathetic hero of one such, the Infante Don Luis of Spain, had, in an excess of enthusiasm, inflicted permanent injury on a sailor of the Montmartre fleet. Since His Highness had also been peddling drugs, he was sent back to Madrid.

Proust, Gide and Cocteau hardly ever went to Montmartre, although once an incident in the quarrel between the last two did take place in the Boulevard Rochechouart, opposite the Cigale music hall, which had been leased by the Soirées de Paris. One of Cocteau's plays was in rehearsal there and Gide came frequently to wait for his young friend Marc Allegret, who was secretary to the Soirées de Paris, at a pavement café there. He was not at all pleased by Allegret's admiration for Cocteau. One day in May 1924, Cocteau, in a fit of anger that the *Nouvelle Revue Française* had failed to publish an article of his, came out of the theatre and insulted Gide. Not waiting for Allegret, not making any response to this furious outburst, not even paying his bill, Gide swept off with a swirl of his cloak down the Rue des Martyrs.

When the typescript of *Our Lady of the Flowers* began to circulate among Cocteau's circle in 1944 it was found to contain both Jésus la Caille and Jean Lorrain's characters, transmuted by a strange poetry. The author, Jean Genêt, after haunting Pigalle in the thirties, had a thorough knowledge of the world of the male prostitute. *Our Lady of the Flowers* is set almost entirely between the Place Blanche and the Place Clichy and opens with the funeral of an aged, painted gigolo, Divine, in the cemetery of Montmartre. Divine had started out in the Place Clichy:

That evening, in Montmartre, she was on the prowl for the first time. Without result. She came on us without warning. The café's regulars had no time to guard their reputations or their womenfolk. Having drunk her tea, Divine writhed her way indifferently – it seemed to look at her – amid a spray of flowers, strewing frills and sequins from invisible flounces, out and away. So here she is, having made up her mind to go home, floating on a cloud of smoke, to her attic, to the door of which is pinned a huge, faded artificial rose. . . . Montmartre was afire. Divine passed through its multicoloured flames and then, intact, stepped back into the darkness of the pavement of the Boulevard de Clichy, a darkness that is kind to the poor faces of the old and ugly. It was three o'clock in the

Oscar Wilde by Toulouse-Lautrec, 1895. Vienna, Private Collection

Portrait of Jean Lorrain in 1895 by Antonio de la Gandara

morning. She walked a bit towards Pigalle. She smiled and stared at every lone man who passed her by. They lacked the courage, or else it was she who was ignorant of the proper forms: the client's doubts, his hesitations, his lack of confidence as soon as he approaches the boy he wants.

In the end Divine did find a 'man', a Corsican pimp called Mignon, who got her such good customers that she became famous among her kind: 'the three Mimosas (a dynasty of Mimosas reigned in Montmartre after the triumph of the great Mimosa, high-flyer of all the frillies), Queen Oriana, First Communion, Bec de Canne, Clairette, Epaissie, the Queen of Rumania'. Divine has two real lovers, a drug-taking negro, Gorgui, and a beautiful young man called Our Lady of the Flowers who ends by murdering an old man. Pimps, drug traffickers, gigolos and more or less corrupt police throng the pages.

At the top of the Rue Lepic is this little cabaret, the Tabernacle, where they practise witchcraft, consult the cards, read tea leaves, where pretty butcher's

William Rothenstein: *Portrait of Verlaine*. Private Collection

boys may be metamorphosed into princesses with flowing trains. The cabaret is small and low-ceilinged. Every Thursday the latch on the little door is shut upon the inquisitive and excited bourgeois customers. We were at home. A gramophone. Three waiters served, eyes full of a lewd mischief. Our men play poker. And we dance. Our habit is to come dressed as ourselves. It is all dressed-up queens and child-pimps, not a grown-up anywhere.

Genêt abandoned Montmartre after *Our Lady of the Flowers*. His novel is the faded sheaf of flowers dropped in the Boulevard de Clichy on the site of the famous *vespasiennes*. The last literary echoes of the pederasts' Montmartre appears here and there in the work of a great Catholic writer, a regular visitor to a house of assignation not unlike the one Jupien laid on for the Baron de Charlus. The mistress of the establishment, an exceedingly respectable-looking lady of some sixty years, is said, on the day when, at the age of eighty, the great writer bade farewell to love, to have filled the room with flowers like an altar.

22
UTRILLO AND COMPANY

Out of all the houses that are left of old Montmartre, there is one filled with memories which has, happily, become its museum. It is to be found at 12 Rue Cortot and has the slightly countrified air of an old farmhouse turned into an artists' lodging. Entering from the north, you go through a terraced garden full of flowering shrubs and bounded by a field planted with vines. On the street side, a projecting arm of the building with a large *porte-cochère* conceals a flower-filled courtyard. Beyond is an unpretentious house probably built during the Restoration on to what in the early eighteenth century was the house of the actor Rose de Rosimont. There, for the first twenty years of this century, lived Emile Bernard, who, from being the friend of Gauguin and the great hope of the school of Pont Aven, turned his back on modern painting, spent long periods in Venice and then came to live in Montmartre. Above his door he wrote: 'Emile Bernard pupil of Titian.' In point of fact, Titian would not have been very proud of his pupil. Bernard covered large canvases extremely competently with more or less allegorical paintings of exotic figures and giants after Michelangelo. However he could talk admirably about painting and would bring all principles round to his own. It was his misfortune to see Gauguin's work growing greater while his own descended into the twilight of provincial museums.

The peaceful atmosphere of the Rue Cortot was disrupted for a good many years when, in 1900, Suzanne Valadon moved in to number 12. Nobody ever washed her dirty linen in public so spectacularly. And, God knew, she had plenty of it. Domestic rows, quarrels with the neighbours, comings home drunk in the early hours of the morning: it was an endless round of shrieking and singing. We have met this magnificent and trying woman before, entering the lives of Puvis de Chavannes, Renoir and Lautrec. We have yet to mention, among her collection of famous names, her affair with Erik Satie. Satie was living in a room in the Rue Cortot, so tiny it was known as the cupboard, and his noisy fights with Suzanne frequently attracted the notice of the police.

After this, tiring somewhat of the uncertainties of bohemian life, Suzanne Valadon married a rich bourgeois, a Monsieur Mussis. She was to be seen driving through the Butte in a tilbury drawn by a pony, a sickly child by her side. 'He is Puvis's son!' she would say proudly. But he was more probably the son of a Spanish art critic named Utrillo, who had lived with Suzanne and thought fit to acknowledge little Maurice some years after his birth in 1883. Suzanne's studio was always too full of people for anyone to take much notice of the child. She had taken Degas's advice and begun to paint seriously, and now she too had models and, naturally, slept with them. One day, the child came upon his mother sprawled on the divan with the biggest of them. He ran away, horrified, to the bistro on the corner where the proprietress, his only friend, gave him a glass of brandy to calm him. This may have been the start of Utrillo's alcoholism, and certainly everything conspired to drive the boy to seek refuge in wine. His martyrdom began when his mother set up house with her favourite model, André Utter, a working man turned painter, and not a bad one at

The Maquis, pastel of about 1890

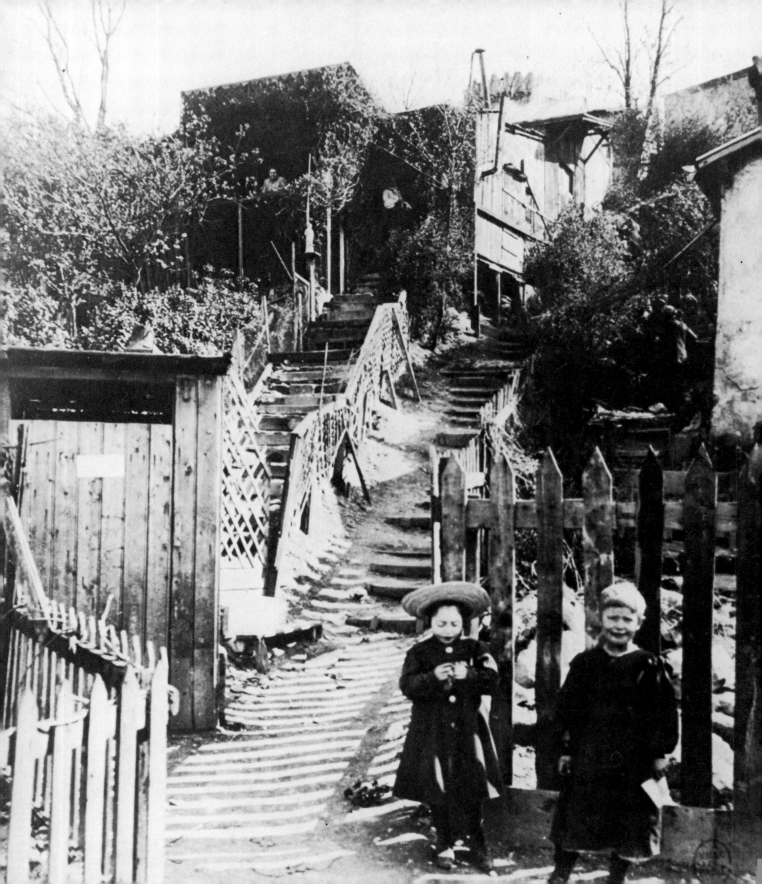

Self-portrait by Emile Bernard at the time when his studio was in the Rue Cortot

that, when it came to pastiches of the different styles being essayed at the time. Maurice, who had done nothing at school, tried various trades but was soon sacked for his drinking. Then, on the advice of a psychiatrist, his mother taught him to paint and he would daub little landscapes of Montmartre. He got some hints from Quizet and imitated Raffaelli to some extent. His progress was so rapid that his mother sent him along to Père Soulier in his paint shop. He gave him some tubes of white, red, green and blue and a little bottle of spirit. 'You've got enough there, my boy, to paint a masterpiece!' And off the young man went to paint the Place du Tertre and then the sad streets with brick buildings on either side and a glimpse of the Sacré-Cœur at the far end. The small boys, who regarded him as a kind of village idiot, would run after him and beat him up. He was beaten at home, too, when he came in drunk; the Rue Cortot would resound to Suzanne's shrieks. The cabaret owners felt sorry for Utrillo and hung his canvases on their walls and one day the art critic Octave Mirbeau, who had done so much for the Impressionists, devoted an article to the unhappy Maurice.

The Maquis. This area is now the slums on the north-west slope of the Butte. Photograph of about 1900

Le Petit Journal

ADMINISTRATION
61, RUE LAFAYETTE, 61

Les manuscrits ne sont pas rendus

On s'abonne sans frais
dans tous les bureaux de poste

5 CENT.   SUPPLÉMENT ILLUSTRÉ   5 CENT.

22me Année — ** — Numéro 1.100

ABONNEMENTS

SEINE et SEINE-ET-OISE . 2 fr.   3 fr. 50
DÉPARTEMENTS . . . . . 2 fr.   4 fr. »
ÉTRANGER . . . . 2 50   5 fr. »

DIMANCHE 17 DÉCEMBRE 1911

LE VIEUX PARIS S'EN VA

Démolition d'un des derniers moulins de la Butte Montmartre

One of the last windmills being pulled down in 1911

(*right*) Utrillo: *Le Lapin Agile*. Avignon, Musée des Beaux-Arts

After that his paintings began to find purchasers and this changed his life, but not for the better. From now on, he was not allowed to idle. He had to work. Suzanne Valadon found that the easiest thing was to shut her son up and make him copy postcards of Montmartre. At the end of the day they would let him drink a few litres of wine. Utter took efficient control of his relations with the picture dealers. 'This is the best thing in a hundred years,' he would say frankly. Every now and then they were obliged to put the painter in a mental asylum and while there, being of a mystical disposition, he would paint cathedrals; since these were not great sellers he was very soon brought back to Montmartre.

Utrillo is one of those painters who make their own forgeries by dint of repeating themselves. Most of the Utrillos that come on to the market are no more than expensive postcards, capitalizing on the myth of Montmartre: stunted trees, crooked houses, the sail of a windmill against a dark sky, muffled human figures in the snow. Then, every now and then, the magic works: lilacs like those in the Rue Cortot burst into bloom along the fences and the dome of the Sacré-Cœur takes on something of the look of St Mark's in a Guardi.

But if the Rue Cortot, with its low houses and gardens spilling over their thick walls, has retained a kind of charm, there is little left of the subjects of Utrillo's best pictures. Young Maurice's playground, a little to the west, a constantly recurring motif, gave way in the twenties to blocks of luxury flats and studios for successful artists. The Surrealist Tristan Tzara had built a block of flats there with money belonging to his wife, a rich Swede. It was here, in the Avenue Junot, that Suzanne Valadon and Utter, thanks to the money earned by Utrillo, moved into a pretty villa. They were ending their days in comfort when a Belgian businesswoman, Lucie Valore, came on the scene and also began to exploit Utrillo. She took him right away from Montmartre to the thoroughly bourgeois suburb of Le Vésinet, where he died in 1955. It was a long time since the painter had walked in Montmartre although the fame of his work captured its picturesque qualities and even prevented some parts from being pulled down. But are we really right to deplore the disappearance of that huge tract of waste land known as the Maquis? Little garden plots on the hillside, some cottages built out of wattle and daub, a few caravans with chimneys added, a scrap dealer's store, brick cottages side by side with boarded shelters: it all added up to a sort of shanty town inhabited by rag-and-bone men, painters, tramps and a few eccentrics like the old English couple who kept goats. Children were everywhere, all more or less in rags. They acquired a measure of celebrity in Poulbot's sketches, for he gave them a mixture of innocence and wickedness which, all in all, made good savages of them. In springtime, with the fruit trees in blossom and the lilacs, and washing of all colours stretched to dry between the houses, with big clumps of iris growing up between the steps, the Maquis could look very pretty. We know that Van Gogh painted several sketches of it. But most of the time it was a sinister place.

Picasso: *Moulin de la Galette*, 1900. New York, Private Collection

Severini: *Pan pan à Monico*. Paris, Musée d'Art Moderne

23
PARIS BY NIGHT

The period between the wars speeded up the commercialization of Montmartre. From bohemian it became frankly sordid and the demolition of the old Montmartre left nothing more than a stage set for the tourists. Carl Van Vechten, who had been very much in love with Montmartre at the age of twenty, went back again in 1930 and wrote with some bitterness:

> I strolled around to the Place du Calvaire to find the whole aspect of the place changed. The exploitation of the Place du Tertre and the picturesque side streets has filled the district with professional postcard sellers in velours berets and jackets and shops where cheap souvenirs are sold. A most unattractive group is now delighted to sit at the tables which occupy all the space in the Place du Tertre. The old Montmartre has completely disappeared.
>
> *(Sacred and Profane Memories)*

The great American Bohemia of Hemingway and Scott Fitzgerald and Djuna Barnes had moved to Montparnasse.

Although the great painters were dead or gone, the singers churning out the same old songs and the pretty girls given way to the most commonplace professionals, the myth of Montmartre was drawing more and more visitors.

> It is a place for everyone to dream of whenever they are oppressed with toil or trouble or riches, the New York banker in his office, the Argentine landowner in his hacienda, the German industrialist in his factory, the people's commissar in his cell, the Chinese camprador on his opium mat. A place which distance, memory and an extraordinary, magnetic reputation endows with every kind of light and charm, and it is called Montmartre. Why have these few hundred square metres, once the haunt of painters and other bohemians, become, since the turn of the century, a symbol of all the magic of the night? Why do the lights in the Place Blanche and the Place Pigalle and the streets that run down and across from them shine out every night like beacons summoning the whole world?
>
> *(Nuits de Montmartre)*

That passage by the journalist and novelist Joseph Kessel comes from the preface to a series of tales set in the Milieu. The Milieu is the world of those who live by prostitution or by drugs, by mixing with gangsters or keeping in with the police. There have always been plenty of Corsicans in the Milieu – although in the last ten years or so there has been a tendency for them to be replaced by Algerians. Political scandals, such as the Staviski affair, of which there were many towards the end of the Third Republic, were often set against the background of the Montmartre cabarets owned by one clan of the Milieu or another. Like a good journalist, Kessel takes us, with his nose for news, from the tramps' doss-house to the night club kept by Russian exiles where everyone wears evening dress.

Théatre de Montmartre. Today it is L'Atelier which was built under the Restoration

In the twenties, the grand tour meant simply the tour of the night clubs, a kind of marathon ritual which no foreign visitor remotely on the ball could possibly miss. Evelyn Waugh was one such. He began in a cellar called the New York Bar, went on to a lesbian café, Le Fétiche, then to La Plantation, where the girls were from Martinique, by way of the Music Box, where they drank very bad champagne in semi-darkness, paused at the luxurious Schéhérazade to eat grilled mutton *à la cosaque*, then on to the Kasbek, another Russian one, and finally to the Brick Top, kept by a drunken American woman. After that, of course, they wound up the night by going down to Les Halles to eat onion soup. 'It was during about the third halt in the pilgrimage I have just described that I began to recognize the same faces crossing and recrossing our path. There seemed to be about a hundred or so people in Montmartre that night, all doing the same round as ourselves.' (*A Pleasure Cruise in 1929*)

Two nudes by Pascin

There is nothing sadder than pleasure when it becomes an industry and it seems unlikely that strip-tease clubs that stay open from three in the afternoon until three in the morning will ever find their Toulouse-Lautrec. Yet there were two very brilliant cartoonists in the twenties who specialized in night clubs. Their names were Chas Laborde and Pascin. The first was a French Grosz but with less savagery. Following Gavarni, Forain and Bottini, Chas Laborde shows us the girls of Montmartre dancing the Charleston and drinking with their clients. But now they have their rivals in the society women 'doing the night clubs' after a dinner or a theatre, who, in unfair competition, are either surrounded by rich men or even stealing their gigolos from the girls.

Pascin had at the same time more talent and less technique than Chas Laborde. He was a Bulgarian Jew, a neurasthenic and a drug-addict, brought up in a brothel, who found himself taken back to his childhood by the atmosphere of cabarets at four o'clock in the morning, when customers and hostesses alike sit slumped over a half-empty bottle, torn between sleep and the desire to have an orgy. The orgy became a way of life in the twenties, when Paul Morand wrote: 'Love has become such a bore that it's only tolerable if there are several of you.' While going the rounds into the small hours, Pascin would pick up girls past their best, and of every colour. They would move in with him for varying lengths of time, but when he wanted young things he would go to a certain Madame Bravo, the cloakroom attendant at a dance hall called La Sevilla. Pascin hanged himself in his studio in 1930, after first slashing his wrists.

To get an idea of the look of the Montmartre streets before the war, it is best to look at the posters which plastered the walls and fences of the remaining pieces of waste ground. It is true that we are a long way from the gaiety of Cheret or the power of Steinlen but those signed Cappiello or Paul Colin do convey the last blaze of the spectacle of Montmartre, the great revues at the Moulin Rouge, turned into a music hall in 1924, with Mistinguett or Raquel Meller singing *La Violettera*, while bunches of violets descended from the chandelier. For fifteen years, the Moulin Rouge had a rival in the Casino de Paris, which was more luxurious still. Then there were the shows at the Bal Tabarin. The great star of Montmartre between the wars was the singer, Damia. Her voice was unequalled, except by Edith Piaf, but she was very beautiful and asked poets like Francis Carco and Mac Orlan to write her songs for her. The atmosphere of a *bal musette*, reminiscences of the Foreign Legion, all the furtive, sentimental life of the Milieu. She had no need of a microphone to make herself heard in the huge halls and her long white arms illustrated her songs to perfection. In a frankly lubricious style, Fréhel, a fat, red-haired woman with a white powdered face, black satin blouse and red scarf, recalled the models of Lautrec.

One of the best theatres in Paris was the pretty Restoration one, directed by Charles Dullin, called L'Atelier. There, in 1922, Cocteau's *Antigone* was put on for the first time, with sets by Picasso and costumes by Chanel. As we have seen, Cocteau

Une saison d'art printanière

"Les soirées de Paris" à la Cigale

Le rideau, peint par Picasso

Picasso's curtain for *Les Soirées de Paris*

played an active part in the Soirées de Paris organized by Count Etienne de Beaumont at the Cigale in the Boulevard Rochechouart. At that time the smartest audiences in Paris invaded this third-rate music hall. The ballets of Milhaud and Poulenc were created there, with sets by Derain and Braque. Cocteau did an adaptation of *Romeo and Juliet* there. One night, the Surrealists, angry with Satie for agreeing to sets by Picasso's great enemy, Picabia, started a fight. With his great height and ringing voice, the Comte de Beaumont commanded riots and ovations alike. Afterwards everyone who was anyone would go on to supper at Graff's. Incidentally, in another theatre in the Boulevard Rochechouart, the Gaîté Lyrique, the great Spanish dancer, Argentina, danced *Love the Magician* by Manuel de Falla.

The Cigale music hall. One of the rare Art Nouveau buildings in Montmartre

The Gaumont Palace. It was built on the site of the Hippodrome

But all these events belonged to Paris and only happened to take place in Montmartre; they owe nothing to its legend. On the other hand, those who still cherished a *nostalgie de la boue* found Montmartre too commercialized and hurried off to the *bals musettes* round the Bastille or even to the suburban dance halls whose atmosphere has been captured so well in some of Marcel Carné's films. The fact was that Montmartre was no longer anything but a memory, growing fainter every day. While it is easy in Ferrara or in Delft to picture the painters who made those small towns famous, it is only in a very few narrow streets in Montmartre that one can still capture the charm that held Van Gogh or Renoir. The haunts beloved of Toulouse-Lautrec and Jean Lorrain have vanished or, like the Moulin de la Galette, fallen into decay.

Yet it is still possible to find some pretty walks over the Butte, along the thick retaining walls, shored up by baulks of timber, that hold back the gardens in those narrow streets ending in steep flights of steps. Here and there some houses a little too heavily restored, a flower-filled square, are signs of a resistance to the destruction. It is no longer permitted to knock down old houses or put up blocks of flats. Two convents have rescued some old houses and their gardens; and there is a Committee for Old Montmartre, housed in a Second Empire pavilion, to guide those visitors who want to get away from the Place du Tertre and the package tours and make a more genuinely artistic pilgrimage.

Yvette Guilbert's gloves by Toulouse-Lautrec

ACKNOWLEDGEMENTS

The author would like to express his gratitude to the Musée du Vieux Montmartre, which so very kindly allowed him to make use of its extensive fund of posters, prints and photographs. The illustrations on the following pages were supplied by the museum: 6, 10, 12, 14, 15, 16, 17, 20, 22, 24, 25, 27, 30, 32, 40, 42, 46, 47, 48, 49, 50, 52 *bottom*, 54, 56, 57, 58, 66, 75, 76, 80, 82, 83, 84, 85, 86, 91, 96, 98, 99, 108, 118, 120, 122, 123, 124, 125, 126, 128, 130, 131, 133, 140, 142, 147, 150, 151, 154, 156, 157, 162, 166, 167, 168, 174, 176, 177, 178, 186, 188, 189, 190, 192, 196, 197.

The publishers would like to thank all those who gave permission for photographs to be reproduced. Photographs were supplied as follows:

Bulloz, Paris: page 78

Chicago, Art Institute: page 153

Giraudon, Paris: between pages 14–15, 174–5, 190–1

Hazlitt, Gooden & Fox: page 146

Lyon, Musée des Beaux-Arts: page 79

George Morrison Archives, Dublin: pages 70, 101, 132, 133, 172

Phaidon Press Archives: between pages 30–1, 35, 36, 44, 60, 62, 64, 68, 72, 73, between 86–7, 92, 93, between 94–5, 102, 103, 104, 105, 106, 107, 109, 110–11, 112, 113, 114, 116, 119, 136, 144, 145, 148, 152, 155, 159, 160, 161, 180, 183, 184, 185, 200

Mr Grégoire Tarnopol, New York: page 52 *top*

Works by Emile Bernard, Pierre Bonnard, Edgar Degas, Jean Louis Forain, Antonio de la Gandara, Pablo Picasso, François Poulbot, Pierre Auguste Renoir, Maurice Utrillo, Suzanne Valadon, Kees Van Dongen and Leon Adolphe Willette are © by SPADEM, Paris. Works by Marie Laurençin and Amedeo Modigliani are © by ADAGP, Paris.

LIST OF COLOUR PLATES

INDEX